the 5:2

COOKBOOK

100 RECIPES *for* FASTING

ANGELA DOWDEN

hamlyn

Angela Dowden is a registered nutritionist who writes on diet and health for numerous newspapers and magazines. She was awarded the Nutrition and Health Writer/Broadcaster of the Year award in 2012.

An Hachette UK Company
www.hachette.co.uk

First published in Great Britain in 2013 by
Hamlyn, a division of Octopus Publishing Group Ltd
Carmelite House, 50 Victoria Embankment, London, EC4Y 0DZ
www.octopusbooks.co.uk

This edition published in 2017

ISBN 978-1-84601-567-0

A CIP catalogue record for this book is available from the British Library

Printed and bound in the UK

10 9 8 7 6 5 4 3 2 1

Both metric and imperial measurements are given for the recipes. Use one set of measures only, not a mixture of both.

Standard level spoon measurements are used in all recipes
1 tablespoon = 15 ml
1 teaspoon = 5 ml

Ovens should be preheated to the specified temperature. If using a fan-assisted oven, follow the manufacturer's instructions for adjusting the time and temperature. Grills should also be preheated.

This book includes dishes made with nuts and nut derivatives. It is advisable for those with known allergic reactions to nuts and nut derivatives and those who may be potentially vulnerable to these allergies, such as pregnant and nursing mothers, invalids, the elderly, babies and children, to avoid dishes made with nuts and nut oils.

The Department of Health advises that eggs should not be consumed raw. This book contains some dishes made with raw or lightly cooked eggs. It is prudent for more vulnerable people such as pregnant and nursing mothers, invalids, the elderly, babies and young children to avoid uncooked or lightly cooked dishes made with eggs.

CONTENTS

The 5:2 diet

Introduction

If you've picked up this book you may already be a convert to intermittent fasting. Alternatively, you may have heard about its benefits and are wondering whether to give it a go. At the other end of the scale you may be a battle-weary diet sceptic, still holding out a small hope you'll one day find the way to shape up and feel healthier permanently. Whatever your starting point or motivation, if you have a small or large amount of weight to lose and would like to feel more comfortable in your own skin, it's for you too.

So what is the 5:2 approach to weight loss and how does it work? There are any number of ways people practise intermittent fasting, from one day of light eating a week to no food at all for several days in a row. The 5:2 approach works well for most people because it's a pragmatic solution that steers a safe, doable and yet effective path through these extremes.

How to use the book

The 5:2 plan allows normal eating (including treats and meals out) for five days a week and then restricts calorie intake for the other two. Until recently, 500 calories for women and 600 calories for men was the 'norm' that most people tried to stick to on fast days. But the good news is that as more has been learnt about 5:2, it's now generally accepted that up to 800 calories – for both men and women – can help people lose weight successfully. For most people, it's the perfect compromise that allows for socializing, family life and work commitments, while still introducing enough calorie control to make sure you lose weight at a healthy rate.

With its delicious and innovative recipe selection, this book shows just how easily you can make 800 calories keep the hunger wolf from the door and, yes, even tickle your taste buds at the same time! It also includes some sweet treats, but they are perfectly suitable for a fast day as they're not too high in sugar.

Ultimately, you'll be losing weight – as can only ever be the case – by eating, overall, fewer calories than your body uses up. But where the 5:2 diet is particularly brilliant is how marvellously achievable it can make this task for food lovers. People who find success with 5:2 often report that they failed to lose weight in the past because cutting back every day was such a struggle – doing so for just a couple of days a week, albeit more drastically, is a much more attractive proposition.

Better still, far from being a short-term fad, those who practise intermittent fasting find it is a lifestyle choice that they can stick to because it doesn't take over their whole life, doesn't demonize specific foods and can even run alongside other supportive weight-loss regimens, such as online food diary methods.

As to the health benefits? As you lose body fat and get trimmer, you can expect to greatly reduce your chance of having a heart attack or developing heart disease. And, in strands of research unrelated to the weight-loss benefits, there's a growing groundswell of science that shows that periodically putting your body into a fasted state – particularly for unbroken stretches of more than 12 hours – may cause various chemical changes linked with lower risk of age-related diseases and higher chance of living healthier for longer.

Whether you're a 5:2 fan in search of food inspiration, or just intrigued to know more, you'll find something in this book for you. Read, digest, get slimmer and enjoy!

IS THE 5:2 DIET FOR EVERYONE?

Most overweight adults can benefit from a 5:2 diet, but it should never be embarked on by children or adolescents, for whom any form of nutritional stress is undesirable. Also, do not do the 5:2 diet if any of the following apply (check with your medical practitioner if you are uncertain).

- You are pregnant, trying to get pregnant or breastfeeding.
- You are already at the bottom end of your healthy weight. You can check this using an online Body Mass Index (BMI) calculator (see page 38) – a BMI of 20 or less would indicate you are not a candidate for 5:2, or indeed any weight-loss programme.
- You are an elite athlete or in training for a marathon or other big stamina event (although normal levels of activity can be undertaken on the 5:2 diet – see page 32).
- You are diabetic.
- You have irritable bowel syndrome
- You have been diagnosed with an eating disorder, either recently or in the past.

How does intermittent fasting work?

People have fasted – out of choice or through necessity – for millennia, so the general concept is far from new. Interest was roused in the 1930s (and repeatedly since) when scientists found that restricting the calories fed to various animals and insects increased their lifespan. The idea of severely restricting calories every other day – rather than by a smaller amount every day – came later, in 2003, with laboratory research carried out at the National Institute on Aging (NIA) in America. The concept of intermittent fasting – and more specifically the 5:2 diet – for managing weight reached a mass audience when Dr Michael Mosley presented the theories in a BBC *Horizon* programme aired in August 2012.

The IGF-1 advantage
Most people are more than happy with the tangible benefits – a flatter stomach and streamlined thighs – that intermittent fasting can bring. But experts are interested in what it may do to our internal chemistry, in particular a hormone called IGF-1, or insulin-like growth factor. IGF-1 is important for growth when we are young but, in adulthood, lower IGF-1 levels are better, as they are linked with a less rapid turnover of cells and, potentially, a decreased cancer risk.

What's been discovered is that fasting can lower levels of IGF-1 and that a modest protein diet (as opposed to a typically meat-packed western one) can have this effect too. IGF-1 levels don't stay depressed for long when you return to normal eating, so the repeated on/off pattern of intermittent fasting might help keep levels persistently lower and healthier. It's a fascinating area of research with lots still to be discovered!

Fasting is nothing new!
Fasting for physical wellbeing and spiritual reflection is as old as the hills and all of the big religions, such as Judaism, Buddhism, Christianity and Islam, embrace it. It's only in modern times that we've become obsessed by the notion that we'll grow weak and depleted if we don't graze on food around the clock. In fact, you don't have to think too long about it to realize that a menu of regularly spaced meals and snacks is probably more alien to our body than periods of feast followed by periods of famine. For cavemen and women, there would undoubtedly have been periods when they

were subsisting only on berries, roots and leaves until the next animal kill, when they were able to stock up on concentrated calories ready for further lean times ahead.

Nowadays, despite being bombarded with never-ending eating opportunities, our bodies are still designed with a biology and hormones that expect food to be scarce at some times and more plentiful at others. This is why many scientists believe intermittent fasting could be a particularly healthy and physiologically appropriate way to keep trim and fight ageing.

As well as suiting our biology, intermittent fasting also works well on a psychological level. The 'carrot' of being able to eat without depriving yourself for five days a week far outweighs the 'stick' of two tougher days each week.

Extending the food-free window

As research around intermittent fasting has progressed, a new way of tackling 5:2 has emerged, which involves the extra element of fitting your meals into an 8–10-hour time eating window. The theory goes that we can benefit from an extended 14–16-hour food-free period overnight because it means we get a rest from processing incoming fuel, helping to keep blood glucose and insulin levels lower for longer periods, which in turn may help with controlling weight and reducing diabetes risk.

Research by biologist Satchin Panda and colleagues at the Salk Institute in California found that mice following a diet did not become as obese (even on exactly the same calories) if they ate over an 8-hour period, rather than grazing all day. And while blood pressure, blood glucose and blood cholesterol went up in the snack-all-day mice, these measures stayed lower and healthier in those animals who ate only during a constricted time period.

Whether this is applicable in humans is not at all certain, and it may be that if you eat healthily (and don't gorge on fatty foods like the mice did) the benefits may not show up. But there is certainly no harm in giving it a go. In practice, an 8-hour eating window might mean not having breakfast or brunch until 11 and finishing your evening meal by 7pm. A 10-hour eating window – more practical for most – means you could stop eating at 6pm and breakfast again at 8am. This 'window' approach to eating can be used on fast days and non-fast days alike, as regularly as is practical given your own circumstances.

Addressing 5:2 diet concerns

Although intermittent fasting diets and 5:2 are now mainstream, you may still have some concerns if you've only ever eaten or dieted in a more conventional manner. To put your mind at rest, some of the most common worries about the 5:2 diet are dealt with below:

FASTING MAY BE OKAY FOR MEN, BUT ISN'T IT BAD FOR WOMEN?
The basis of this argument seems to be that women have lower lean tissue levels and as such have less reserve if skipped meals lead to the breakdown of essential muscle. Even if this were a concern – and studies of moderate intermittent fasting regimes suggest it's not – this is covered by eating modest amounts of protein on your fast day (see Fast Day Eating guidelines on page 19). Another small study that compared the experiences of eight non-obese men and women might also seem a blow to women, as it concluded that intermittent fasting seemed to 'adversely affect glucose tolerance in non-obese women but not in non-obese men'. However, the subjects were on a harsh regimen with no food at all for 36 hours in every 48-hour period. Obese women following much gentler routines, like the one advocated in this book, show very good responses in blood glucose levels and markers of diabetes risk (see page 13).

DOESN'T 'FASTING' ENCOURAGE EATING DISORDERS?
We're very clear that you shouldn't try intermittent fasting if you have ever had an eating disorder. This is just to be safe in case it unearths any old obsessive behaviours. More lengthy forms of fasting may be somewhat addictive but 5:2 isn't a food-free fast at all, it's just a restricted-calorie one. There is no evidence at all that it can trigger a new eating disorder.

ISN'T SKIPPING MEALS BAD FOR YOU?
If skipping meals is part of a generally erratic and unhealthy pattern of eating, where you lurch from one unhealthy snack to another in lieu of proper balanced meals, then yes. However, with the type of controlled food restriction advocated by 5:2, the focus is on getting good nutrition despite having very few calories. There's now also lots of evidence showing that, far from being bad for you, periods with no or very little food intake are actually healthy, provided, as outlined on page 7 and above, you don't have a medical or psychological condition that prohibits it.

HOW ABOUT BREAKFAST?

The need to eat breakfast for better health and weight control has been rammed into us! But if it works for you to leave eating until later on a fast day (or indeed a non-fast day) you can absolutely do that – in fact doing this may offer benefits as already described. While there is a correlation between breakfast eating and better health, the former probably doesn't directly cause the latter. Instead, breakfast eating is likely just a marker for better behaviours in general – breakfast eaters may be less likely to smoke or eat a lot of saturated fat for example.

ARE 5:2 REGIMENS STRICT ENOUGH TO GET MAXIMAL HEALTH BENEFITS?

One criticism, usually from academic quarters, is that 5:2 fasting doesn't actually deliver as many health benefits as it could and that periods of 18–36 hours without food are needed for potential protection against conditions like Alzheimer's and cancer. This is at odds with what's conventionally thought safe and sensible, so is there a sensible compromise? If you want to potentially maximize the benefits of 5:2, one way may be to extend your food-free window, as detailed on page 9. However, fasting in any prolonged fashion is beyond the remit of this book, and the focus of our 5:2 advice is safe and efficient weight loss, so never do anything that feels uncomfortable.

CAN IT AFFECT SLEEP AND STRESS LEVELS?

There have been some reports that fasting can lead to people sleeping more fitfully or feeling more anxious, which may be linked with changes in blood sugar level. However, such side effects are much more likely to occur with intense fasting programmes than they are with the more moderate 5:2 regimen, especially this one that allows you a fairly generous 800 calories on fast days.

WILL I NEED VITAMIN SUPPLEMENTS?

5:2 does not advocate the cutting out of any foods or food groups, and so is less likely to leave you short of nutrients than more faddy regimens. If you use 5:2 as an opportunity to overhaul your eating habits for the good, there should be even less reason to need supplements. However, some people, women in particular, can find that nutrient intakes become borderline when they cut calories. If you do choose to take a supplement make it a basic A–Z style one.

The health benefits of intermittent fasting

As with any emerging new science, intermittent fasting attracts a variety of expert opinion and debate, but what's undeniable is that the research into the health benefits of intermittent fasting is really picking up. Although to date the number of human studies may have been rather small, this is rapidly changing, with new results coming out all the time.

So what do we know are the benefits of intermittent fasting so far?

Inflammation

Inflammation is more than just the swelling or redness we experience in response to an allergy or injury. Low level chronic inflammation (which is made worse by poor diet and being obese) is now thought to play a role in very many diseases from arthritis and asthma through heart disease, type 2 (adult onset) diabetes and even cancer.

A healthy diet that's low in saturated fat and rich in fresh fruits and vegetables, whole grains and healthy fats (like those found in oily fish), can help dampen inflammation. But there's also evidence that intermittent fasting can help reduce levels of inflammation. Researchers at Yale School of Medicine found that a compound called ß-hydroxybutyrate (BHB), which is produced by the body during periods of intermittent fasting, can inhibit the action of a complex set of proteins (the inflammasome) that is key in driving the inflammatory response.

Weight loss

When you eat no more than 800 calories for two days a week and don't significantly overcompensate during the remaining five days (as evidence shows most people don't), it stands to reason that weight will start to fall off. But research suggests that intermittent fasting may help people remove excess weight in a more efficient and effective way than normal calorie restriction.

In particular, a 2011 review by researchers at the University of Illinois at Chicago found that people who did alternate day fasting (a repeating pattern of one day unrestricted eating followed by one day of no- or low-calorie fasting – see also page 38) were more likely to retain higher amounts of muscle tissue while losing at least as much fat. This is important because muscle helps to keep your metabolic rate higher, in essence because it is much more metabolically active than other tissues. In short, by having a more muscular frame you can continue to burn more calories all day every day, even when you are resting, which is very helpful in managing your weight over the longer term.

What doesn't kill you makes you stronger

Research published in the *Journal of Nutritional Biochemistry* showed that feeding rats and mice only every other day improved the health and function of their brains, hearts and other organs. Other studies have shown that mice and rats on intermittent fasts develop fewer cancers, are less prone to neurological disorders and live 30 per cent longer than their siblings that were fed every day. All this is fascinating stuff that's driving the new wave of human studies, but what's particularly interesting is that experts think it's the *stress* that fasting puts on the body that does the good!

According to Professor Mark Mattson – the world's most cited neuroscientist as reported in *New Scientist* magazine – fasting is a type of hormesis, a process whereby organisms exposed to low levels of stress or toxins become more resistant to tougher challenges. For example, the mild biological stress induced by fasting causes cells in the heart and gut to produce proteins that decrease heart rate and blood pressure and increase gut motility (the movement of food through the gut), reducing the risk of heart disease, stroke and colon cancer. It really does seem to be a case of what doesn't kill you (i.e., managing on minimum food for a couple of days a week) makes you stronger!

Diabetes and blood sugar control

Any amount of weight loss in obese individuals, however it is achieved, will generally result in the body becoming more sensitive to insulin, which is an important step towards reducing the risk of diabetes (exercise has the effect of making you more responsive to insulin, too). But intermittent fasting could have a particularly good effect on your blood sugar control and diabetes risk.

In Dr Michelle Harvie's studies at the Genesis Breast Cancer Prevention Unit at Manchester's Wyntheshawe Hospital, women on a 5:2-style low-carbohydrate, high protein fasting diet (consuming up to 650 calories for two days each week, and a Mediterranean-style diet for the rest of the time), have been compared with women restricted to 1,500 calories every day. In both groups women lose weight, reduce their cholesterol levels, record lower blood pressures and have reduced markers of breast cancer risk. When it comes to reductions in fasting insulin and insulin resistance – both signs that diabetes risk has decreased – the benefits are greater in the 5:2 diet group than those using conventional calorie restriction.

Heart disease

As already alluded to, a reduction in cardiovascular risk factors – for example, LDL cholesterol (that's the 'bad' type that carries cholesterol towards arteries, where it collects and causes 'furring') and high blood pressure – can be expected on the 5:2 diet. Triglycerides in the blood will also tend to fall as you lose weight (put simply, this means that your blood is less sticky and therefore less liable to clot).

Much of the work in this area has been done by Dr Krista Varady and her team at the University of Illinois at Chicago, with one of her scientific papers on the subject being entitled 'Intermittent fasting combined with calorie restriction is effective for weight loss and cardio-protection in obese women' (November 2012). The research outlines the benefit that intermittent fasting, and wider, healthy weight loss, can contribute to a healthy heart. It's all very much in the title really!

Brain function

Much of the research into intermittent fasting actually started, and continues, in the healthy ageing field, and brain ageing in particular. At the National Institute on Aging in America they've been investigating rats and mice that have been genetically engineered to develop Alzheimer's disease. Given normal circumstances, these animals show obvious signs of dementia by the time they are a year old (getting disorientated in a maze that they have previously been able to navigate with ease, for example), but when they're put on an on/off fasting regimen they don't develop dementia until they're around 20 months, or much nearer the natural end of their lives.

What could be the reason? One thing that's been reported is that the fasting mouse brain produces more of a protein called BDNF (brain-derived neurotrophic factor), which stimulates the growth of new nerve cells in the hippocampus part of the brain, essential for learning and memory. There's certainly an evolutionary logic for the fasting state to be linked with better cognitive function, too: if you were hungry in caveman days, you needed your wits about you to track down the next meal and survive!

As yet there are still many unknowns (for example, whether longer periods of fasting are needed than normally experienced on a 5:2 diet) and the human studies have still to be done, so it's impossible to say if intermittent fasting will help to prevent dementia. But it's certainly a very interesting area of research, and one to watch.

Cancer

Much of the published research into the potential disease-protective effects of intermittent fasting involve measuring a biological marker named insulin-like growth factor-1 (IGF-1), which is known to be associated with cancer. Fasting has the effect of reducing IGF-1 levels, at least temporarily, and also seems to stimulate genes that repair our cells.

How a reduction in IGF-1 translates into successful real-world outcomes (i.e., a reduced chance of people getting cancer) is still unclear, however. One 2007 clinical review did look at 'real-world' health outcomes and concluded that intermittent fasting (specifically, alternate day fasting, which usually has minimum 18-hour periods without food) may have a protective effect against cancer, as well as heart disease and diabetes. However, it concluded 'research is required to establish definitively the consequences', which is a fair reflection of the science as it currently is. In short, how effective intermittent fasting is against cancer relative to other healthy-eating or weight-loss regimens is still to be clarified.

COULD 5:2 MAKE YOU HAPPIER?

Anecdotally, many 5:2 eaters say their low-calorie intake makes them feel more clear-headed, more able to concentrate and even more cheerful. It's uncertain as to why this should be, but feeling more upbeat will certainly make it easier to refuse that slice of cake!

Getting started

The beauty of the 5:2 diet is that, beyond the requirement for two 800-calorie days a week, there are no firm rules and it's very flexible. As with all new healthy habits, however, it can take time to adjust and the hunger aspect can initially be hard. On the plus side, the results you begin to see and feel within short order mean your fast days will quickly become less of a chore, and even something you can begin to enjoy. Preparation and planning are key.

Choose your fasting days

As a first step, you'll need to decide which days will work best for you as fasting days. This may evolve over time, or from week to week, according to your circumstances. As a general rule, you're more likely to stick to the regimen if you can repeat the same two days every week, so try to choose days that you'll need to deviate from only infrequently. For example, don't pick a Tuesday if this is the day when a friend is most likely to invite you round for lunch, or a Friday if you're going to be tempted by a takeaway after work. For obvious reasons, weekend days may not be such good fasting days either, but everyone's different and you should choose what works for you.

Whether you run the two days consecutively or apart is also up to you, and there isn't enough research to say definitively that one way or another is best. Most people doing 5:2 for themselves, rather than in the context of a highly monitored clinical trial, simply find it easiest in terms of managing hunger and keeping on track to have a gap between fasting days. However, if two days together suits you better, and you feel energetic and motivated, there's no reason why you shouldn't do it this way.

WHY UP TO 800 CALORIES?

5:2 dieters have traditionally eaten only 500–600 calories a day on fast days, and if this amount works for you, then great! But the good news is that having up to 800 calories can have similar results. This new figure of 800 is at the upper end of what counts as a VLCD (very low calorie diet) – used by the medical profession for decades to rapidly reduce weight and associated health risks. Having the flexibility to go up to 800 calories on your two fast days makes 5:2 much easier.

Fast day meals

The second decision to make is how you will spread your 800 calories over the fasting day. Again, this is down to personal preference, usually honed through trial and error. A satisfying format for many people is to have a 600–700 calories spread between brunch/lunch and dinner, with 100–200 calories left over for snacking, perhaps during the afternoon.

One argument for leaving your first calorie intake until lunch or later is that the stretch of time you go without food is longer – perhaps 14 hours or more – which some researchers have surmised may be associated with potentially bigger health benefits (see page 9). If you are the type of person that can't get going without a good breakfast first thing, by all means move your first meal earlier in the day, but consider stopping eating earlier the night before to extend your overnight food-free window.

Some 5:2 dieters (usually men, on anecdotal evidence) prefer saving up their 800 calories for just one good-sized evening meal and that is also fine should you prefer this.

On the other hand, many people, perhaps women in particular, prefer to graze their way through fast days, and Dr Michelle Harvie's research offers some reassurance here. It found that obese women eating three small, evenly-spaced mini meals on two non-consecutive fasting days per week lost weight efficiently and also reduced levels of inflammatory chemicals that increase breast cancer risk.

The main point is to find what suits you and not to shoehorn yourself into a routine that doesn't fit your lifestyle. We simply don't know the optimum food-free stretch, if there is any optimum at all.

To find a pattern of food intake that enables you to stick to your 5:2 plans and achieve sustainable weight loss, try keeping a food and mood diary. Making a note of how you feel physically and mentally on fast days can be an effective way to track how well you're coping with the regimen. Simply jot down what foods/meals you eat, when you have them and any accompanying feelings of hunger, mood or wavering willpower. Registering when you feel at your weakest and strongest on a fast day can help you to tailor future fast days so that they are easier.

Is less than 800 calories better if I can manage it?

With the updated 5:2 you can have 800 calories on fast days, but that isn't a 'rule' that you should or must obey. It's best to think of it more as 'up to' 800 calories and if you feel comfortable consuming less, then do so, though you should never go lower than 500 calories a day if you're a woman, or 600 calories if you're a man.

On the basis that successful weight loss is always about creating a deficit between calories consumed and calories used up, you might experience marginally faster weight loss if you stick to 500 calories rather that 800 but the reality is that the more you go below 800 calories the more effort you put in for only a relatively small increase in reward. Having the leeway to go up to 800 calories might be the difference between sticking to 5:2 or not.

WHAT DOES 800 CALORIES LOOK LIKE?

As a rough guide, 800 calories would be:

- Breakfast/brunch: 1 large poached egg and a grilled tomato on a medium slice of wholemeal toast spread with a 7 g scrape (scant teaspoon) of butter; 100 g (3½ oz) blueberries with 100g (3½ oz) 0% fat Greek yogurt (358 calories)
- Snack/light lunch: Medium banana (81 calories)
- Dinner: A can of ratatouille topped with a 120 g (4 oz) portion (raw weight) grilled or microwaved cod and a scattering of 100g (3½ oz) cooked, peeled prawns (357 calories)

TOTAL 796 calories

Depending on where you are starting from and your current habits this might seem like a surprisingly satisfying amount of food or not much at all. If it doesn't seem enough don't worry – there are lots of tips for making your fasting day as painless as possible in the following pages. While most intermittent fasters will find it challenging at first, the process gets much easier as your body adapts.

Fast day eating

Theoretically you could have a large burger and endless cups of black coffee on a fast day and be within your calorie allowance, but clearly this wouldn't be at all good for you! Instead, it's a great idea to use your fasting day to make balanced and healthy choices, using the following guidelines.

Eat five a day
Your fast day is the perfect opportunity to fill up on fruit and veg as these foods are bulky and low in calories, take up plenty of room on your plate (a psychological boost!) and are linked with a lower risk of killer diseases such as heart disease and cancer. Green leafy vegetables, such as spinach, kale, watercress, rocket, broccoli and cabbage, are particularly low in calories, as are berries, such as strawberries, raspberries, blackcurrants and redcurrants, which you'll often find in convenient form in the freezer section of the supermarket. Tomatoes, peppers, orange-fleshed melons and butternut squash join the low-calorie corner – the wonderful thing about all these richly coloured fruit and veg is they consistently appear in superfood lists because of their high antioxidant content (antioxidants are the component in fruit and veg that mop up the free radicals that can damage our cells).

In short, by using your fast day as a chance to eat at least five colourful portions of fruit and veg a day (a portion is around 80 g/ 3 oz, or roughly a handful), you'll be boosting your health as well as benefiting your waistline.

Dairy and pulses
These two deserve a special mention because they're unusual in providing a combination of carbs and protein in one easy package and are a great source of vitamins and minerals. They can be easy on the waistline too – 0% fat Greek yogurt (a great topping for fruit) has only 57 calories in a 100 g (3½ oz) serving, while creamy canned butter beans (fabulous to bulk out a salad) have 56 calories in a 60 g (2½ oz) serving.

Include lean protein
The lowest calorie lean protein sources (all weighing in at less than 100 calories for a 100 g/3½ oz portion) include prawns, tofu and tuna canned in water, though grilled fish, eggs and chicken breast are also

very good choices. Including one or more of these protein foods on a fast day is to be recommended, as you're more likely to preserve valuable muscle tissue during periods of calorie restriction when protein is consumed (and particularly if you exercise, too). Another big bonus is that protein is particularly good at keeping you full, so can help to keep hunger pangs at bay for longer. Digesting it also uses up more calories than does digesting other nutrients, which is all grist to the mill of your diminishing middle!

Choose quality carbs

Admittedly you won't be able to eat very big carb portions on a fast day (there are around 100 calories in just one slice of bread, for example), but it's a good idea to make sure any modest portions you do choose are as unprocessed or nutrient rich as possible, and to focus on higher fibre choices where you can. Wholemeal breads, porridge oats, wholewheat pasta, pearl barley, fortified wholegrain breakfast cereals and potatoes in their skins tend to have a relatively low glycaemic index or GI, which means they raise blood sugar levels only relatively slowly, helping to keep blood sugar, energy and appetite levels more controlled.

Perhaps more important, though, is *not* to spend too many (if any) of your fast day calories on sweet and sugary carbohydrates, such as biscuits or dessert. (A rough rule of thumb would be to use no more than 75–100 calories on these foods.) Quite apart from their lack of nutrient value, they'll really challenge your ability to stay on track because they can cause your blood sugar levels to fluctuate, heightening feelings of hunger.

PERFECT FAST DAY PROPORTIONS

- Concentrate on fruit and veg (steamed, grilled, stir-fried or in soups and salads) as your main stomach-filling priority (filling half your plate).
- Fill the other half of your plate with low GI carbohydrate-rich and/or protein-rich foods.
- Any calories you have left over you can use as you wish (see the lists of up to 50, 100 and 150 calorie snack suggestions on pages 44–6). But choosing more nutritious foods is always best.

Drink options

It is important to stay well hydrated on fast days (see page 33), but with the exception of low-fat milk (or a milk alternative, such as soya milk), many drinks can be a wasteful, non-filling way to spend calories. Your best options on a fast day are calorie-free drinks, such as black coffee and tea (though try not to drink more caffeine than you would normally), herbal teas, diet drinks and of course (and best of all), good old water. To jazz it up, try a sparkling variety and add a squeeze of lime or lemon.

Alcohol is one of the least sensible choices of all (even the smallest glass of wine has around 100 calories and could stimulate your appetite) so use your fast days to abstain from alcohol altogether and give your liver two days a week of much needed rest!

TOP TIPS FOR BEGINNERS

- The day before your first fast, eat well and aim to go to bed feeling neither hungry nor overfull. Getting an early night is good preparation. Trying to stuff in as much food as late as possible so you don't feel hungry tomorrow is not!
- Do your eating homework so that you know how you are going to spend your 800 calories, and which meals you are going to spread them between. Use the recipes in this book as inspiration and make sure you are stocked up with the requisite ingredients.
- Try to make your environment as devoid of food temptations as possible, which means ensuring a stray slice of pork pie isn't the thing screaming, 'eat me!' when you open the fridge.
- Arm yourself with some kind of calorie counter – there is one to get you started on pages 152–7 – or you can use an online app or website.
- Be aware that choosing a less busy day to start your fasting may not be the best approach. As long as you have your food choices pre-planned, a day with plenty to keep you occupied may be better.
- If you find your first fast too hard and have to give in, you've probably just chosen the wrong day. Don't despair and try again another time, but leave it a few days.

Fast day feel-full tips

• Water is the perfect slimline filler, either drunk on its own to temporarily take the edge off a hunger pang or, more particularly, incorporated within food to increase satiety (the feeling of fullness that food imparts). Chunky soups plus lots of fruit and veg can work particularly well on a fast day because they'll help to make your stomach feel full.

• Airy foods take up more space on your plate (so, psychologically, it feels like you're being presented with more food), as well as in your stomach. One study by Professor Barbara Rolls at Pennsylvania State University, published in the journal *Appetite*, compared the same snack in a puffed and non-puffed version and found that those receiving the airy snack ate 73 per cent more in volume, but consumed 21 per cent fewer calories. Rice cakes are the ultimate airy food, and a whipped mousse (which can have fewer than 80 calories per pot) is the way to go if you really can't do without dessert!

• Protein-rich foods are particularly good at inducing satiety. One theory is that they stimulate the release of hunger-controlling hormones in the gut. The protein in eggs seems particularly good at keeping you full, so give them a try!

• Wholegrain versions of breakfast cereals, breads, pasta, rice and noodles take longer to chew and are more satisfying, as the fibre they contain provides bulk but no calories. Fibre also has a slowing effect on the passage of food through the gut, which has the effect of keeping you fuller for longer. The portion size of bread or pasta you can have on a fast day is small, but choosing a brown, not white, version can help to make it more filling.

• Focus on whole foods. On average, foods that aren't highly processed, pre-packaged or high in sugar will tend to be lower GI and keep your blood sugar levels on a more even keel.

Don't estimate!

Building up an accurate picture of what actually constitutes 800 calories (see the box on page 18) is one of the most educational and interesting aspects of the 5:2 diet. It can help you understand what constitutes a healthy portion and might also give a clue as to why you ended up needing to lose a few pounds in the first place.

It won't come as a surprise, then, that 'estimates' and 'educated guesses' are definitely not okay when it comes to calculating your fast day calories. With the best will in the world you'll almost certainly be wrong, which will jeopardize your weight loss and dilute the health benefits. If you're not convinced, try seeing if you can correctly estimate the 'recommended' 30 g (1 oz) serving of flake-style breakfast cereal, such as bran flakes. Most people pour nearer to 50–60 g (2–2½ oz) into the bowl, which can add over 100 'accidental' calories and completely destroy a fasting day.

If you don't own weighing scales and a measuring jug, you need to lay your hands on both. With a basic set of electronic kitchen scales available at relatively low cost, and measuring jugs even cheaper, it doesn't require a great investment. Make sure you also have some measuring spoons in your kitchen drawer and you'll be well fixed.

At first, you should weigh everything until you've got a clearer idea of what different-sized portions weigh. Your idea of a 'medium-sized' apple – 100 g (3½ oz) with peel but no core, according to official publications – may be very different to mine or someone else's. It's also important to weigh the ingredients carefully when you're making the recipes in this book, so they don't exceed the calorie counts given.

If it seems like a pain, it's really not – it's actually quite fun learning about calories and portion sizes and, as you're only doing it two days a week and you're not eating terribly much on those days either, it's not at all onerous. Look at it as a chance to really understand what you are putting into your mouth.

WHAT ABOUT SWEETENERS?

Sugar substitutes, including aspartame, sucralose and more recently stevia, have been approved by the UK government and health authorities the world over, yet there still seems to be a host of scare stories circulating as to how they could actually make us fatter or even cause cancer. In the end it's up to you if you want to use them or not, but if adding a bit of sweetness to a bowl of berries or to a cup of tea makes you more inclined to stay on track with your 5:2 diet, then go ahead and use them. Unless you're eating sweeteners in vast quantities they are very unlikely to do any harm and are a much better bet on fast days than spoonfuls of sugar.

'Off' day eating

Of necessity, some time has been spent explaining about fasting days, what to eat on them and how to make sure they're successful. But let's not forget that the beauty of 5:2, and the core reason that it appeals to, and works for, so many people, is that you can have five days each week without worrying about cutting a single calorie!

Does that mean you can truly eat anything you want too? Well, yes, but naturally there are limits. The good news? Studies consistently show that contrary to what you might expect, intermittent fasters are actually very unlikely to go on a big binge on their 'off' days. Rather than make your appetite more extreme, 5:2 dieting seems to help naturally regulate it so you enjoy only as much food as you need when you aren't fasting. That said, if your journey to 5:2 eating has involved a lifetime of flip-flopping between failed diets and bingeing, it may take longer for a healthy relationship with food to develop.

Am I hungry, am I full?

While 5:2 fasting can ultimately help you regulate your food intake and weight without micro-managing every mouthful, the thought of genuinely being able to eat what you want for five days a week may seem a little scary at first. If so, you may need a little hand-holding until you can get to a point where you trust your eating intuition.

One simple technique that can help is to regularly rate your hunger on a scale of 1 to 10 throughout the day. On this scale, 1 is ravenously, stomach growlingly hungry, whereas 10 is completely stuffed to the point of discomfort. As the ideal is for you to feel reasonably hungry before a meal and comfortably satisfied afterwards, the aim is not to start eating until you register 4 or below on the scale, and to stop putting food in your mouth when you hit 7 or 8.

Chewing thoroughly before swallowing, putting your knife and fork down between bites and taking at least 20 minutes over a meal are all other great tips to help you slow down, notice and appreciate what you are eating and naturally self-regulate your food intake.

Is it head hunger?

Over time, your fast days will help teach you what it's like to feel physically hungry, so you can distinguish between when you need to eat and when you only have an urge to do so. Here are a few ways you can distinguish between head hunger (fake) and stomach hunger (real).

HEAD HUNGER
- Is something you're likely to experience in association with negative emotions like frustration or anger, or as a response to stress, boredom or habit.
- Is non-hungry eating, stimulated by the likes of food adverts on TV.
- Will be experienced as something like a nagging voice in your head, convincing you that you're having a bad day so it's fine to eat.

STOMACH HUNGER
- Is a physical sensation – your stomach rumbles and feels empty.
- Is still there and stronger 20 minutes after you distract yourself with a non-food-related activity.
- Only usually happens three or so hours after your last proper meal, dependent on what you ate.

Balanced eating

If you do feel like you need the security of calorie counting on 'off' days, the best advice is to stick to around 1,900–2,000 calories if you are a woman and around 2,400–2,500 if you are a man. This would be the average 'weight maintenance' level of calories if you were entering your food intake into a weight-loss website.

'Off' days have plenty of scope to include treats (see box below), but non-fast days should include a good balance of wholesome foods, too. As a guideline, ideally the following food groups should be included daily to ensure you get the nutrients your body requires. This is not a lecture about foods you *must* eat – just some helpful hints, should you need them, on how to eat well.

WHAT DOES 2,000 CALORIES LOOK LIKE?

As a guide, 2,000 calories might look something like this:

- Breakfast: Poached egg, two grilled bacon rashers, grilled tomato and mushrooms, small glass of orange juice
- Lunch: Chicken salad sandwich, pot of fruit yogurt, grapes and melon slices
- Dinner: Chilli con carne, broccoli and carrots, small serving of apple crumble
- Snacks: Packet of crisps, finger-style chocolate biscuit bar

FRUIT AND VEG

As with your fast days, try to include five different portions of fruit and veg daily for their fibre, vitamin, mineral and antioxidant content. As a rough guide, a portion is approximately the amount you can hold in your hand. All types (excluding potatoes) count, including fresh, frozen, canned, dried and juiced.

CARBOHYDRATES

As with fast days, minimally processed, wholegrain or high-fibre types (for example, wholemeal bread) are best, but this doesn't mean you can't also have white bread, oven chips or naan occasionally if you want to. At the average meal, these starchy carbohydrate foods should ideally take up around a quarter of the space on your plate to help provide the energy, B vitamins and fibre your body needs.

PROTEIN

At an ideal meal, protein would take up another quarter of your plate, about the same size as the carb serving. Protein is needed for muscles

CAN I EAT A HIGH-FAT DIET AND STILL LOSE WEIGHT?

As it happens, you can! In a fascinating study published in the January 2013 edition of the journal *Metabolism – Clinical and Experimental*, alternate day intermittent fasters lost similar amounts of weight, including from around their waist, whether they got 45 per cent of their calories from fat, or a more abstemious 25 per cent. Both groups also showed reductions in cardiovascular risk factors, including blood levels of cholesterol and triglycerides. Of important note, though, is that subjects in the trial did not eat more calories on the high-fat regimen.

And while people who have been used to high-fat diets may be able to stick to intermittent fasting better if they continue with the fatty foods they love, the authors say it's not such a good idea for your heart health long term. A moderate-fat diet of up to 35 per cent of calories from fat is fine, however (and is about what Britons currently eat). So much the better if you swap some of those fats from the saturated to the unsaturated kind – so less butter, cream and processed meat products, and more nuts, seeds, vegetable oils, avocados and oily fish.

and tissues to grow or repair themselves, and it's also wonderfully satiating. On your 'off' days you can focus less on choosing proteins simply according to their calorie content and leanness, and this affords greater opportunity for choosing more eco-friendly, sustainable sources. These tend to be the plant proteins – for example, beans, pulses, nuts, Quorn and tofu.

DAIRY OR ALTERNATIVES
Including dairy foods or fortified alternatives, such as soya, rice, oat, almond or hazelnut milks, makes it easier to make sure you get enough calcium in your diet. In turn, this helps to keep bones strong. There's some evidence that people with dairy- or calcium-rich diets find it easier to manage their weight, too – another good reason to regularly include these foods.

Watch those portions!
An important aspect of 5:2 is that you don't have to feel bound by any eating rules on your 'off' days. However, supersized portions are worth a special mention because they are so prevalent and can really distort our perception of what is an appropriate amount to eat.

COFFEE
Once, a standard serving was perhaps a 200 ml (7 fl oz) cup of instant coffee (about 45 calories with milk and sugar). Now, the smallest size in coffee shops is at least 354 ml (12 fl oz) and it's not unusual to see coffee sizes up to 590 ml (1 pint). Opt for a medium mocha coffee with semi-skimmed milk and whipped cream, and you'll be downing 315 calories – more than a McDonald's cheeseburger!

To beat portion distortion go for basic filter coffee, or at most a skinny latte (102 calories for a 350 ml/12 fl oz size).

HOME-COOKED DISHES
Analysis of recipes in the 2006 edition of the American cookbook, *Joy of Cooking*, found the suggested serving size of identical main courses had increased by as much as 42 per cent from recipes in the first edition in 1931. The effect on dishes like spaghetti Bolognese or shepherd's pie has been to add approximately 150 calories.

To beat portion distortion serve on smaller plates. Moving from a 30-cm (12-inch) to a 25-cm (10-inch) dinner plate leads people to serve and eat around 22 per cent less.

WINE

Most wine glasses used to contain 125 ml (4 fl oz) – about 85 calories and 1.5 alcohol units – but now a 'small' pub or wine bar measure is 175 ml (6 fl oz) – about 120 calories and over 2 units. The largest is 250 ml (8 fl oz), or a third of a bottle!

To beat portion distortion use smaller glasses at home and buy lower alcohol wines of 12 per cent or less. At the pub, stick to one glass!

READY MEALS

A Food Standards Agency-commissioned report found popular ready meals had significantly increased in size. For example, an individual beef lasagne meal morphed from 250 g (8 oz) in 1990 to 320–500 g (11–16 oz) in 2008.

To beat portion distortion check calories per 100 g (3½ oz), which is even more important than size when it comes to ready meals. Less than 150 calories per 100 g (3½ oz) is a reasonable level to aim for on non-fasting days.

POPCORN

According to America's National Heart, Lung, and Blood Institute (NHLBI), the average cinema popcorn serving increased from 270 calories 20 years ago to 630 calories today. Even though you could leave those extra 360 calories behind, you probably won't.

To beat portion distortion always opt for the smallest bucket size even if it doesn't seem good value for money.

FAST FOOD

America's NHLBI says an average pizza serving has 850 calories today compared with 500 calories two decades ago. Burgers are also bigger – when McDonald's first began in 1955, its only hamburger patty weighed around 45 g (1¾ oz). Now, it's not uncommon to have two quarter pounders (250 g/8 oz) in one bun, while a Big Mac (490 calories) is actually on the small side compared with many burgers!

To beat portion distortion choose a burger that's no bigger than your balled fist, and opt for small fries. If a pizza is more than 25 cm (10 inches) across, share it.

What to expect on the 5:2 diet

If you have a BMI of 25 or more (to check your BMI, see page 38) when you start your 5:2 eating plan you can expect to lose weight at an average rate of 500 g (1 lb) a week until you stabilize at a healthy weight within the 18.5–25 BMI range. However, as with any form of calorie restriction, the amount you lose will vary from week to week, so expect highs, lows and plateaus along the way. In the beginning you may lose weight quite quickly – 1–1.5 kg (2–3 lb) isn't unusual in the first week – which can be hugely motivating. The flipside is that you risk becoming despondent in the weeks that follow if your weight loss fluctuates or slows down. The key to success is always to have the bigger picture in mind – there may be disappointments along the way, but all the evidence suggests that in the longer term you will succeed. While the path may not be entirely smooth, no other slim-down regimen can boast that you can eat normally for five days a week and still be 6.35 kg (14 lb) lighter in three to four months.

Measuring your progress

Before you begin the 5:2 diet, it's a good idea to know what your starting point is so you can measure your progress along the way. Some people say they prefer not to use scales and are happy just to measure their progress in terms of a looser waistband, but this can often be about denial. No one is forcing you to weigh and measure, but if your weight has been creeping ever upwards and you haven't been tracking it, it is probably best to bite the bullet, get on those scales and face up to what your starting point may be.

MONITORING YOUR WEIGHT

Research findings from America's National Weight Control Registry – a database of people who have maintained a weight loss of 13.6 kg (30 lb) or more for at least one year or more – show that 75 per cent of weight-watchers use regular weighing as part of their success strategy, and most diet and health professionals now believe that weekly monitoring of weight is a marker of diet success.

Many bathrooms scales will also give you a read-out of your percentage body fat, which should show a pleasing downward trend as the weeks go by. Do be aware that different scales can give quite different body fat readings, however, and even the same scales will register ups and downs from one day to the next, depending on factors such as time of day and how much fluid you've consumed. As with your weight, it's the trend over time that matters, so don't get hung up over individual measurements.

WAIST MEASUREMENT
Another simple but effective way to measure your progress is with a tape measure around your middle. Measure at the place where your waist is naturally narrowest or, if this is hard to define, at the midpoint between the top of your hip bone and the bottom of your ribs. This measurement is a reasonable proxy for the amount of internal fat you have in the central region and in turn a good marker for heart disease, high blood pressure and diabetes risk. As your waist measurement falls, your risk of developing any of these conditions is steadily reduced.

For men, risk moves from high to medium as waist measurement falls below 102 cm (40 inches) and to low risk when the measurement goes below 94 cm (37 inches). For women, the respective figures are 88 cm (34½ inches) and 80 cm (31½ inches). People of Asian backgrounds tend to have a higher proportion of body fat to muscle and need to achieve smaller waist measurements than those of Caucasians to achieve the same level of risk reduction.

AVAILABLE TESTS
As you progress with 5:2 fasting and the weight continues to drop off, you can also expect your level of LDL cholesterol (see page 14) to decrease, your blood pressure to come down and your blood glucose level to shift downwards. Other biomarkers – for example, those that predict cancer risk (see page 15) – will also be likely to improve.

Overstretched medical practitioners tend not to be best pleased when 'worried well' patients demand repeated tests for no good medical reason. And less run-of-the-mill blood tests – for example,

EXPECT FOOD TO TASTE WONDERFUL!

One thing that 5:2 eaters consistently report is how delicious even simple flavours taste on fast day. When you're not constantly eating, the delayed gratification that's associated with being properly hungry makes you really appreciate your food. Fresh vegetables, lean meat and subtle natural flavours really come into their own. Because you know your meals are very limited, your taste buds seem heightened and you will savour every bite, taking time over each morsel. People who had previously always shunned vegetables often start eating piles of them with 5:2, which can only be a good thing!

for IGF-1, which has been tracked in some intermittent fasting trials – aren't available in the UK on the NHS. However, your health care practitioner may be happy to do simple but important checks on your blood pressure and cholesterol level, both now and after you've lost about 6.5 kg (14 lb) or so. If not, some pharmacies offer a fully validated cholesterol check, which is relatively inexpensive.

Dealing with hunger

At first, those gripey hunger pangs can seem quite insistent on fast days. But the good news is that those feelings definitely become much less intense, with most long-term 5:2 devotees stating that they are no longer unduly troubled by fast day hunger after a few weeks. Another possibility is that intermittent fasters simply learn to embrace the feeling and not to be fazed by it.

Getting on top of initial hunger pangs can be as simple as actually experiencing those feelings and realizing that you can come out the other side without collapsing in a heap on the floor or dying of starvation! We're so programmed to eat at the slightest twinge of hunger that feeling anything more than slightly peckish can actually be quite alien and even a little bit scary. In time, when you realize nothing dreadful is going to happen if you feel hungry for a day, this will change and you can actually learn to appreciate the physical sensations of hunger you get on a fast day, knowing that you are in tune with your body and have tackled the art of being able to savour food without overloading your system.

However, if you're struggling in the early stages, here are some tips for riding out hunger pangs:

• Be aware that the pangs often come in waves – although you may be particularly hungry now, you probably won't be in 20 minutes if you focus on something else.
• Write a list of simple activities that will distract you from thoughts of hunger (anything from phoning a friend to cleaning your shoes). Pin it to the fridge as a reminder for times when you start to weaken.
• Go for a run or walk, whichever suits you. It's one of the best ways to temporarily distract yourself from hunger.
• Brushing your teeth straight after your evening meal on a fast day makes it less likely that you'll succumb to evening munchies. Best of all, get an early night, as you can't eat when you are asleep!

Exercise and 5:2

An exercise programme can definitely complement your 5:2 weight-loss progress, and will provide many attendant health benefits, such as stronger bones and a healthier heart.

But how should you negotiate exercise on a fast day? The old wisdom was that you should be well fuelled prior to exercise but the latest evidence suggests that modest activity in the fasted state is actually good for you. In particular, exercising in the fasted state means that the body has to use fat as its primary fuel, which is good news for the disappearance of those love handles! Another benefit of exercising on an empty stomach appears to be that you'll build muscle better when you do get round to eating in the post-exercise period.

In a nutshell, there's no reason you shouldn't work out on your fast day, with the ideal being to exercise when you are feeling hungry, perhaps in the afternoon, and then to follow with one of your fast day meals.

However, common sense must come into play and if you're new to exercise it's probably best to ease yourself into physical activity on non-fast days only. There's also some suggestion that women are better doing weights on fasting days (while men can particularly benefit from cardio work). Listening to your body is essential, and you should always stop exercising immediately if you feel faint, dizzy or light-headed.

HOW ACTIVE SHOULD I BE?

Official guidelines suggest that for optimum health benefits you should be physically active (at the level of brisk walking or gentle cycling, for example) for at least 30 minutes five times a week. If you're doing something more vigorous, such as running or playing a racquet sport, you can get away with 75 minutes, or three 25-minute sessions a week. On top of this, one or two 20-minute sessions with weights are also recommended to maintain muscle tone and lean tissue levels, particularly in the over 40s.

10 ways to make the 5:2 diet work for you

1 Be flexible

The 5:2 regimen is definitely not a prescriptive diet with a big list of 'dos' and 'don'ts' that you may have been used to in the past. That's a plus point, but it can also be a tad off-putting at first if you're used to being told exactly what to do as part of a weight-loss regimen.

The secret to finding the version for you is to be prepared to road-test different fasting day routines until you find the one that works best. When it comes down to it, the chance to change fasting days around is the key attraction of 5:2 and you should feel free to exploit that flexibility to its fullest.

2 Keep well hydrated

Fluid is your friend on fast days as it helps to give a sensation of stomach fullness, at least temporarily. As it's also possible to confuse hunger with thirst, keeping up your intake of fluids at all times will prevent you falling foul of this potentially waist-widening mix-up. As a bonus, water is needed for every chemical reaction in the body, including burning fat.

Don't think you must stick to plain water if you don't want to, though – black tea and coffee, herbal tea and calorie-free beverages all count towards your fluid intake, too.

3 Find a fasting buddy

Research shows that when you're tackling your weight you'll do better if you have someone doing it alongside you. For example, a study at the University of Pennsylvania found that 66 per cent of the people dieting with friends had maintained their weight loss after 10 months compared to only 24 per cent of those who were on their own.

There's no particular reason that you'll need more support with 5:2 than any other regimen, and in fact many people do it quite successfully all by themselves as the periods of food deprivation are short and manageable. However, if a partner or friend wants to do it with you, you should jump at the chance for the extra support it brings.

4 Keep out of temptation's way

Fasting days are surprisingly doable, and with a positive mindset and some forward menu planning you can even sit down for an evening meal (albeit with a different mix of foods on your plate) with the rest of the family. But – and it's a big and fairly logical but – there's simply no point putting yourself in temptation's way if you can avoid it!

Research at Cornell University's Food and Brand Lab in America has identified visibility and convenience as the two biggest drivers of mindless eating, with 'out of sight' being a key strategy to successful calorie control. So taking steps as simple as keeping biscuits in an opaque container or in a drawer, or moving a bowl of sweets from your office desk to a filing cabinet a distance away can markedly increase your chances of staying on track on a fast day.

However, if you are faced with a food temptation, psychologists believe tightening muscles is so closely tied to determination that simply doing it can muster up greater will power to resist. In studies, subjects were more likely to think they could resist chocolate cake while flexing their biceps, while others were better able to resist unhealthy foods at a snack bar while holding a pen woven through spread fingers (thus engaging their hand muscles). It's not hard to imagine how clenching helps, and balling your fists is certainly worth a try when faced with a strong temptation to break your fast!

5 Save chocolate for 'off' days

Quite apart from the fact that you'll only be able to have a disappointingly teeny amount, one small study has suggested that eating chocolate when we are hungry may heighten our general desire for it. Conversely, eating it when we are full may 'train' us out of a craving. Researchers at University College London split students into two groups, giving both groups half a bar of chocolate twice a day. After two weeks, the half that had been told to eat their chocolate rations on an empty stomach reported a stronger craving than before. By contrast, the students who had been eating the chocolate on a full stomach craved chocolate less and even reported that it now seemed somewhat less pleasant to the taste.

6 Consider an internet food shop

Patrolling the aisles with your trolley can give you a small amount of exercise, but you may find that it's better to do an online shop and go for a run instead! The reason? When you're shopping for fast day food, supermarkets can be a toxic environment in the sense that the sights, smells and deli counters can lure you to put things in your basket that you hadn't got on your list and didn't intend to buy. On your five 'off' days, you can of course choose whatever foods you want, but many people do find they start to develop a natural inclination to eat a more balanced and healthy diet overall, which online shopping is potentially more supportive of. Certainly, if your grocery shop starts to involve lots of label reading (often in a challenging font size!), it may be easier to do this food-sleuthing at the click of a mouse rather than in the supermarket itself.

7 Stay positive about weight loss

Virtually all people trying to lose weight will experience phases when they continue to stay at the same weight for what seems like a frustratingly long period of time. In actuality it's likely to be only a few weeks, and anecdotally 5:2 eaters seem to experience fewer plateaus, possibly because of the constant switch between higher and lower calorie intakes and because levels of lean tissue (with a higher energy expenditure than fat) are maintained. However, if you do experience a plateau, a positive mindset is key. Try to focus on the weight you have lost and consider every week that you stick with your fast days as a success that's worth patting yourself on the back for. In reality, it's only plateaus that happen early on that tend to be a problem. Most established 5:2 fans are so wedded to their routine, weight loss becomes purely a bonus. On a practical level, shifting your activity level up a gear can help shake you out of a plateau.

8 Keep busy

The devil may make work for idle hands, but you're also more likely to end up with your hands in the biscuit tin if you're bored or not very busy. Part of planning a successful fasting day is therefore thinking what you will do to occupy yourself as well as what you will eat. The most successful days are those when you have particularly engrossing work project, are focusing on caring for children or (hopefully from time to time) just enjoying a day out.

9 Get more sleep

The evidence that insufficient sleep correlates to higher body weight has been piling up, and the latest strand of evidence suggests junk food may be particularly appealing to tired brains. When scientists at St Luke's-Roosevelt Hospital Center and Columbia University in New York used high-tech brain scans to measure responses to unhealthy foods (like pepperoni pizza and sweets) versus healthier options (porridge and fruit), they found that the brain's reward centre lit up more at the sight of junk food if subjects were fatigued.

The take-home message? Get plenty of sleep, particularly the night before a fast day. At the very least it's good for your general wellbeing; at best it may also help keep up your 5:2 resolve.

10 Don't be hard on yourself

If you have to miss a few fasting days because of holidays or other life events, don't beat yourself up. There's always tomorrow or next week and you're meant to be living a life, not a life sentence!

YOUR RELATIONSHIP WITH FOOD

As time goes by, you can expect your relationship with food to change. Rather than food being your master, as is so often the case with those who have struggled with their weight over the years, you're likely to notice a welcome shift in the locus of control, putting you in the driving seat once more. A frequent comment from people who adopt 5:2 as a lifestyle choice is that when they discover they can 'crack' fast days, it is extremely empowering.

In essence, 5:2 fast days can help you to be more in tune with your body and its appetite and hunger cues. The confidence boost that this gives means a healthier relationship with food can develop. For some people this will be more of an epiphany than others but, regardless of the magnitude of the effect, feeling more in control of your diet is always welcome.

5:2 for life

Once you've reached the weight you're happy with, what next? As you've read through these pages, I hope you've become convinced that intermittent fasting, or 5:2, could well be something you incorporate into your life long term, as an active lifestyle choice. When bigger, longer studies into intermittent fasting emerge, as they undoubtedly will, the optimal way to continue intermittent fasting so that you can maximize any health benefits and keep your weight maintained will almost certainly become more apparent.

For now, the consensus approach from most people doing 5:2 who have already reached their ideal weight and don't wish to become any slimmer is to switch to up to 800-calorie fasting just one day a week (a 6:1 diet!). A small study showed people who had lost weight could keep it off by doing this, though another approach, if you want to keep a slightly firmer watch on your weight, would be to continue with two fast days – but let them creep up to 1,000 calories, say.

Some people may find they can manage by using 5:2 fasting now and again (intermittent intermittent fasting, if you like!), or to stop for longer periods or even altogether. These folk will be the ones who have become confident that they can now trust their own eating intuition to keep them safe from weight gain. In short, they can now trust their inbuilt hunger and fullness mechanisms (that were there all the time!) to stay happily at their optimum weight.

Whatever your approach, remember that you should always obtain pleasure from your eating and your diet should never become a terrible chore. If you choose intermittent fasting as your ongoing method of optimizing health and weight, the recipes and suggested plans that follow should make that eminently possible, for as long as you choose.

Frequently asked questions

How can I check my BMI?

The Body Mass Index (BMI) is an estimate of health risk based on your height and weight. You can use an online calculator (for example, at www.nhs.uk) or work it out using the following calculation. Measure your weight in kilograms, then divide it by your height in metres squared. For example, a woman of 1.6 m (5 feet 3 inches) who weighs 63.5 kg (140 lb) has a BMI of $63.5 \div (1.6 \times 1.6) = 24.8$.

According to World Health Organization guidelines, a healthy BMI is in the range of 18.5 to 25, with health risk starting to rise above this. However, significant health risk probably does not kick in for many until around 35. If you're short or of Asian descent having a BMI above the healthy range is more of a worry than if you're tall or athletic.

How does alternate day fasting compare?

Alternate day fasting is the type more widely researched in humans, and in clinical studies has involved giving individuals meals set at 25 per cent of their needs one day and 125 per cent the next. There are no direct comparisons of 5:2 fasting versus alternate day fasting, but 5:2 is just a logical adaptation that also works, and for very obvious reasons is much less disruptive to people's lives.

Do some 5:2 diets recommend specific foods on fast days?

Yes, they do – the intermittent diet formulated by experts at the Genesis Breast Cancer Prevention charity, recommends that on fast days women follow a high protein low carbohydrate diet with healthy fat and plenty of non-starchy vegetables and fruit. Protein is useful for 5:2 dieters as it helps with satiety, The diet has been proven clinically effective at reducing weight and associated breast cancer risk. Find more details at www.thetwodaydiet.co.uk.

Can I use 5:2 to lose a small amount of weight?

Yes – many people use the 5:2 diet to lose that slight increase in weight that has crept on as they've got older, or to get back to a lighter weight within the normal range that they feel happier with. However, if you only have a small amount of weight to lose, you'll lose it more slowly than if you have a lot to lose. And it goes without saying that you shouldn't lose weight if it's going to move you out of the bottom of the healthy BMI range (see above).

How tough will 5:2 be?

Everyone is different, and it can depend on everything from your genes to your mood on a particular day. The only way is to try it and you may be pleasantly surprised. You do, after all, eat *something*, and it can be surprising how filling 800 calories are when you start making the right food choices. Many people report that hunger becomes less and they no longer get hunger pangs mid morning or mid afternoon once they have been doing 5:2 for a while.

Will my body go into 'starvation mode'?

Starvation mode as it's popularly understood is something of a myth. In the context of most slimmers' experiences, all it means is that your metabolic rate will decrease slightly as your body adapts to consistently fewer calories coming into the system.

Starvation mode is itself never responsible for weight gain (only increasing your calories again will do that) and is only ever really troublesome if you fast or drastically cut calories for long periods, in which case you will not achieve as great a weight loss as you might expect. On a 5:2 diet, the constant shake-up of low and higher calorie days is likely (though not proven) to make starvation mode even less of a problem.

Can a fast day be any 24-hour period?

It could be, and doing from 2 pm to 2 pm is one possibility that some people like. If you do this you can have lunch as your final 'off' day meal and then any combination of dinner and breakfast or lunch in the following 24-hour period as your two fast meals. You have to be sure not to overcompensate with your non-fast meals, though, as the timings can make this slightly more likely.

Won't I be so hungry that I just pig out on my 'off' days?

No, this is not what the scientific evidence or ordinary people's experiences show. Dr Krista Varady, an alternate day fasting expert, expected that her study subjects would eat around 175 per cent of normal calories the day following a fast, but consistently she found this not to be true. Dr Michelle Harvie also found her subjects, on a 5:2 diet, did not overcompensate.

Can I really eat cake on my 'off' days?

No foods are banned, so yes! In fact, you can eat anything you like on either fast or non-fast days but portions will have to be different and you soon learn that junk food calories don't go very far. If you consistently eat high-calorie foods on 'off' days, then you'll get to the point where you outweigh the benefit of fast days, but this doesn't usually happen and the expectation is that you'll naturally start to crave healthier meals and not want to eat cake as much in any case.

Can I have alcohol?

On 'off' days, yes! But it's a bad idea on all sorts of levels on your fast days. Apart from containing a lot of calories, booze can lower your inhibition and self-control, leading you astray much more easily than would otherwise be the case.

Can I follow 5:2 for health and not to lose weight?

Yes, if you want too, but in this case it's probably best to have only one fast day a week. There's some (only scant) evidence that if you're just after the health benefits and not bothered about weight loss, eating all your fast day calories in just one meal at lunch or dinner could be better, to extend the food-free period (see pages 9 and 17). But don't do this if it feels in any way uncomfortable.

Can I sit down and eat with my family?

Yes – for example, you could just have a smaller portion or swap some of the pasta or rice for salad, or any similar trick that keeps you at the right calorie figure. Many of our recipes could be served to all the family with other family members having another accompanying dish. Cooking for other people and being around them when they eat may seem hard but it can be surprisingly manageable when you're suitably focused. Most 5:2 eaters are, because they know that tomorrow they can be tucking in with everybody else.

Just one word of caution if you have children: kids learn food habits from their parents so if you must tell them you're doing something different, explain that you're just enjoying really healthy food to satisfy your appetite rather than being 'on a diet'. Having children is one really good reason to carry through healthier eating habits into your 'off' days, too.

4-week fast day meal planner

Tasty meals are your absolute ally on fast days, so here's a month's worth to get you started (or shake things up a bit if you're getting stuck for ideas). Make sure you are scrupulous with portion sizes when you're serving up the recipes.

Week 1

DAY 1
- **Breakfast/brunch:** ½ plain bagel topped with 30g (1 oz) light soft cheese and 50 g (2 oz) smoked salmon (270 calories)
- **Snack/light lunch:** 1 oatcake spread with a level tablespoon of reduced-fat hummus (91 calories)
- **Dinner:** Thai Noodles with Tofu (see page 140); 3 dates (401 calories)

TOTAL 762 calories

DAY 2
- **Breakfast/brunch:** 1 large poached egg and a grilled tomato on a medium slice of wholemeal toast spread with a 7g scrape (scant teaspoon) of butter (261 calories)
- **Snack/light lunch:** Moroccan Tomato & Chickpea Salad (see page 76) (200 calories)
- **Dinner:** Seared Steak with Parmesan & Rocket (see page 131) (290 calories)

TOTAL 751 calories

Week 2

DAY 1
- **Breakfast/brunch:** 30 g (1 oz) serving of bran flakes with 125 ml (4 fl oz) semi-skimmed milk and 100 g (3½ oz) blueberries (188 calories)
- **Snack/light lunch:** A medium apple, sliced and served with 16 g (about a level tablespoon) peanut butter (156 calories)
- **Dinner:** A can of ratatouille topped with a 120 g (4 oz) portion (raw weight) grilled or microwaved cod; Green Beans with Ham & Garlic (see page 94) (450 calories)

TOTAL 794 calories

DAY 2
- **Breakfast/brunch:** Red Fruit Salad (see page 67) with 100 g (3½ oz) 0% fat Greek yogurt; slice of medium wholemeal toast spread with 7g (a scant teaspoon) of butter (309 calories)
- **Snack/light lunch:** 1 serving of Fennel & White Bean Soup (see page 73) (155 calories)
- **Dinner:** Grilled Sea Bass with Cherry Tomatoes (see page 122), with steamed broccoli and spinach and 70 g; (2½ oz) (2 mini) boiled new potatoes in their skins (330 calories)

TOTAL 794 calories

Week 3

DAY 1
- **Breakfast/brunch:** Porridge made with 50 g (2 oz) oats and 300 ml (7 fl oz) semi-skimmed milk, topped with 100 g (3½ oz) raspberries and sweetener if required (357 calories)
- **Snack/light lunch:** Tabbouleh Salad (see page 77) (193 calories)
- **Dinner:** 2 Lemon Grass Fish Skewers (see page 58) served with a large vegetable 'steam fry' (200 g/7 oz pepper, cabbage, onions and courgettes stir-fried in 1 teaspoon of oil and a few drops of water. Add soy sauce to taste (199 calories)

TOTAL 749 calories

DAY 2
- **Breakfast/brunch:** 1 boiled egg with ½ slice of wholemeal toast spread with yeast extract and cut into a few 'soldiers'; 100 g (3½ oz) blueberries with 100 g (3½ oz) 0% fat Greek yogurt (250 calories)
- **Snack/light lunch:** 300 g (10 oz) shop-bought fresh carrot and coriander soup and 1 smallish apple (about 100 g / 3½ oz) (150 calories)
- **Dinner:** Marinated Pork Fillet (see page 136) and a rocket and cherry tomato salad (40 g/1½ oz rocket, 80 g/3 oz tomatoes) dressed with 2 teaspoons olive oil and a 2 teaspoon drizzle of balsamic glaze (397 calories)

TOTAL 797 calories

Week 4

DAY 1
- **Breakfast/brunch:** 2 slices (60 g /2 oz) of premium dry-cured ham and 2 slices (40 g /1½ oz of Jarlesberg cheese on 2 rye crispbreads; 2 easy peeler citrus fruits (333 calories)
- **Snack/light lunch:** Chicken Salad Thai Style (see page 80 (144 calories)
- **Dinner:** Vegetable Curry (see page 139) served with 100 g (3½ oz) shop-bought cauliflower rice (302 calories)

TOTAL 779 calories

DAY 2
- **Breakfast/brunch:** 1 slice of wholemeal toast spread with 7g (scant teaspoon) of butter and yeast extract, and a 100g (3½ oz) raspberries (184 calories)
- **Snack/light lunch:** Wild Mushroom Omelette (see page 144) (282 calories)
- **Dinner:** 95 g (3½ oz) can skinless, boneless sardines in tomato sauce on a bed of bagged leaves with a baked potato (200 g/7 oz uncooked weight) and 100 g (3½ oz) cherry tomatoes (323 calories)

TOTAL 789 calories

Snacks and treats

15 snacks up to 150 calories

- 80 g (3 oz) slice of 'healthy range' crustless egg and bacon quiche: 129 calories
- 30 g (1 oz) Somerset brie and a 75 g (2½ oz) small bunch of red seedless grapes: 143 calories
- 1 packet of light (reduced-fat) crisps from a multi pack: 115 calories
- 30 g (1 oz) handful of berry granola: 127 calories
- 25 g (1 oz) nuts and raisins: 132 calories
- 40 g (1½ oz) (approx. 2 tablespoons) shop-bought guacamole dip on a rice cake: 128 calories
- 25 g (1 oz) 70 per cent cocoa chocolate: 141 calories
- 3 dates: 125 calories
- 2 mini vegetable samosas (weighing 25 g/1 oz each): 124 calories
- 30 g (1 oz) wasabi peas: 122 calories
- 1 banana and 100 g (3½ oz) fresh pineapple pieces: 138 calories
- Individual pack of breadsticks with cheese dip: 111 calories
- Mini 25 g (1 oz) serving of bran flakes with 100 ml (3½ fl oz) semi-skimmed milk: 138 calories
- 2 mini pittas (17 g/½ oz each) with 30 g (1 oz) light soft cheese: 147 calories
- ½ hot cross bun spread with a tablespoon of reduced-sugar jam: 142 calories

50 snacks up to 100 calories

- 1 medium apple: 53 calories (125 g/4 oz weighed whole)
- 15 g (½ oz) plain almonds: 88 calories (around 9 nuts, but weigh them as they vary)
- 1 warm crumpet spread with yeast extract (no butter): 100 calories
- 15 g (½ oz) salted popcorn: 83 calories
- 100 g (3½ oz) shop-bought lemon and coriander prawns: 80 calories
- 1 slice of Parma ham wrapped around a breadstick: 58 calories
- 1 rye crispbread with 30 g (1 oz) light soft cheese: 82 calories
- 1 individually wrapped mini malt loaf (for lunch boxes): 95 calories
- 50 g (2 oz) (¼ pot) reduced-fat prawn cocktail: 83 calories
- 15 g (½ oz) roasted, salted peanuts: 89 calories
- 1 rounded tablespoon (30 g/1 oz) of tzatziki with 100 g (3½ oz) cucumber and red pepper sticks: 60 calories
- 100 g (3½ oz) fat-free strawberry yogurt: 79 calories
- 1 light cheese triangle and 1 slice of cucumber spread on 1 oatcake: 82 calories
- 1 medium banana: 81 calories
- 200 g (7 oz) canned lentil soup: 95 calories

- 1 falafel with 1 teaspoon of sweet chilli sauce: 65 calories
- 100 g (3½ oz) cooked chicken tikka breast pieces: 100 calories
- 2 cold Quorn mini savoury eggs: 100 calories
- 100 g (3½ oz) blueberries with 100 g (3½ oz) 0% fat Greek yogurt: 97 calories
- 12 g (½ oz) Brazil nuts: 82 calories (2 nuts, but weigh them as they vary)
- 20 g (¾ oz) wafer-thin ham, 1 tomato and a little mustard: 81 calories
- 1 small glass (150 ml/¼ pint) low-fat strawberry milkshake: 90 calories
- ½ pomegranate: 55 calories
- 1 sesame rice cake with 7 g (¼ oz) tahini: 74 calories
- 50 g (2 oz) reduced-fat mozzarella with 80 g (3 oz) sliced tomato: 98 calories
- 1 slice of fruit loaf: 98 calories
- 50 g (2 oz) mashed avocado flesh sprinkled with lime juice: 100 calories
- 50 g (2 oz) reduced-fat hummus with cucumber sticks: 100 calories
- 1 digestive biscuit: 71 calories
- 1 pack of baked cheese-flavour corn puffs from a variety pack: 90 calories
- 1 slice of garlic baguette: 95 calories
- 1 pot of fat-free probiotic yogurt drink and 1 apple (100 g/3½ oz): 78 calories
- 5 small strawberries topped with 2 rounded tablespoons (60 g/2½ oz) of 0% fat Greek yogurt with honey: 83 calories
- 1 fish finger with a serving of ketchup: 80 calories
- 1 mini gouda-type cheese: 61 calories
- 2 cream crackers spread with 1 tablespoon of squeezy guacamole: 84 calories
- 40 g (1½ oz) rocket dressed with 2 tablespoons of low-fat balsamic dressing and 10 g (⅓ oz) grated Parmesan cheese: 71 calories
- 45 g (1½ oz) (¼ deli pot) marinated olives: 85 calories
- 65 g (2½ oz) chunky honey roast ham slices: 98 calories
- 2 clementines and 1 kiwifruit: 73 calories
- ½ slice of toast soldiers dipped into 50 g (2 oz) mild salsa from a jar: 66 calories
- 1 large hard-boiled egg: 84 calories
- 60 g (2½ oz) (½ deli pot) sun-dried tomatoes in oil, drained, served on a bed of salad leaves: 87 calories
- 30 g (1 oz) pistachio nuts (unshelled weight): 86 calories
- 1 medium orange: 59 calories
- 25 g (1 oz) piece of Edam cheese: 85 calories

- 1 mini vegetable samosa: 75 calories (check as they vary)
- 300 g (10 oz) shop-bought fresh carrot and coriander soup: 89 calories (they vary, so check the label)
- 40 g (1½ oz) canned tuna in water mashed with 30 g (1 oz) canned sweetcorn and 1 teaspoon of reduced-fat mayonnaise: 92 calories
- 1 shop-bought lemon and raisin pancake: 88 calories

50 snacks up to 50 calories

- ½ cup (80 g/3 oz) mango cubes: 46 calories
- 1 teaspoon of peanut butter spread on a celery stick: 42 calories
- 1 slice of cantaloupe melon: 23 calories
- 100 g (3½ oz) frozen summer berries with sweetener: 30 calories
- 80 g (3 oz) apple and grape snack pack: 45 calories
- 3 seafood sticks: 50 calories
- 2 clementines: 44 calories
- 80 g (3 oz) crunchy whole carrot: 28 calories
- 1 small apple: 42 calories (100 g/3½ oz weighed whole)
- 14 g (½ oz) miniature pack of raisins: 41 calories
- 100 g (3½ oz) fresh blackberries: 25 calories
- 60 g (2½ oz) fresh unpitted cherries: 23 calories
- 50 g (2 oz) cooked jumbo prawns with a squeeze of lemon: 33 calories
- 1 ginger nut biscuit: 47 calories
- 1 mini light Gouda-type cheese: 42 calories
- 2 slices of wafer-thin ham wrapped round a celery stick: 43 calories
- 1 rich tea biscuit: 38 calories
- 1 oatcake spread with yeast extract: 37 calories
- 100 g (3½ oz) cucumber with 50 g (2 oz) salsa from a jar: 26 calories
- 50 g (2 oz) red seedless grapes: 30 calories
- 100 g (3½ oz) cherry tomatoes: 20 calories
- 2 party-sized chicken satay skewers: 36 calories
- 30 g (1 oz) garlic and herb light soft cheese with celery sticks: 48 calories
- 1 sachet of miso soup: 30 calories (but check as they vary)
- 1 small (50 g/2 oz) pot of fruit-flavoured fromage frais: 49 calories
- 1 kiwifruit: 44 calories
- ½ slice of Danish wholemeal toast spread with 2 teaspoons of salmon paste: 45 calories
- 2 fresh apricots: 33 calories
- 1 cream cracker topped with 10 g (⅓ oz) French chèvre: 65 calories
- 2 Melba toasts spread with 1 level teaspoon of reduced-sugar jam: 34 calories

- 100 g (3½ oz) asparagus spears, steamed, with a shake of chilli flakes: 28 calories
- 2 tablespoons of squeezy guacamole with celery sticks: 32 calories
- ½ medium banana: 41 calories
- 50 g (2 oz) (about 1 heaped tablespoon) ready-to-eat strawberry custard: 50 calories
- 1 cocktail sausage: 26 calories
- 1 streaky bacon rasher: 39 calories
- 1 regular cheese triangle: 42 calories
- 40 g (1½ oz) bistro salad (lamb's lettuce, beetroot and chard) from a bag with 15 g (½ oz) pitted black olives and 1 tablespoon of low-fat French dressing: 41 calories
- 2 Cheddar cheese biscuits: 40 calories
- 1 nectarine: 45 calories
- ½ pink grapefruit, with sweetener if liked: 24 calories
- 1 cheese oatcake: 39 calories
- ½ red or orange pepper, cut into strips: 26 calories
- 2 teaspoons of toasted sunflower seeds: 42 calories
- 1 jumbo cheese-flavoured rice and corn cake: 38 calories
- 6 slices (30 g/1 oz) of bresaola: 48 calories
- 20 g (¾ oz) (2 dessertspoons) pickle with carrot sticks: 48 calories
- 1 mini pork salami sausage: 40 calories
- 2 prunes: 39 calories
- 100 g (3½ oz) ripe papaya flesh: 43 calories

10 guilt-free treats

- 6 medium strawberries with 12.5 g (½ oz) serving of aerosol cream: 85 calories
- 50 g (2 oz) gravadlax with sauce: 97 calories (check as they vary)
- 175 g (6 oz) pot ready-to-eat sugar-free cranberry and raspberry jelly with 80 g (3 oz) raspberries: 33 calories
- 15 g (½ oz) cocoa-dusted almonds: 84 calories
- 1 slice of Parma ham with 3 watermelon balls: 48 calories
- 10 g (⅓ oz) (around 2 lumps) crystallized ginger: 37 calories
- 1 scoop of raspberry sorbet: 64 calories
- 2 mini spring rolls: 90 calories (check as they vary)
- 2 poppadums: 76 calories (check as they vary)
- 250 g (9 oz) shop-bought shell-on mussels in garlic butter sauce: 100 calories (check as they vary)

Recipes

100
CALORIES AND UNDER

Tahini hummus

- 250 g (8 oz) canned chickpeas, rinsed and drained
- 2 tablespoons tahini
- 3 garlic cloves, chopped
- 125 ml (4 fl oz) lemon juice
- pinch of ground cumin
- vegetable stock or water (optional)
- paprika or chopped parsley, to garnish

1 Place the chickpeas, tahini, garlic, lemon juice and cumin in a food processor or blender and process until well blended, adding a little water or vegetable stock if you prefer a thinner consistency. Add more garlic, lemon juice or cumin to taste.

2 Transfer the hummus to a serving bowl and serve sprinkled with paprika or chopped parsley.

Top tip

To prepare for your fast day, shop in advance for all the ingredients you will need and try to make sure that there are no tempting snacks that might lead you astray.

69
CALORIES
PER SERVING

Serves 6
Preparation time 10 minutes, plus cooling
Cooking time 5 minutes

Jerusalem artichoke hummus

- 375 g (12 oz) Jerusalem artichokes, scrubbed
- 50 g (2 oz) butter, diced
- 150 ml (¼ pint) chicken stock
- 250 g (9 oz) canned chickpeas, rinsed and drained
- 1 teaspoon ground cumin
- 2 tablespoons lemon juice
- 1 garlic clove, crushed

1 Cook the artichokes in a saucepan of boiling water for 5 minutes or until tender. Drain and leave to cool.

2 Place the artichokes in a blender or food processor with the butter and stock and blend until smooth. Add the chickpeas, cumin, lemon juice and garlic and blend again until smooth, then serve.

Top tip

Watch out for condiments. Replace ketchup, mayonnaise or salad dressing with balsamic vinegar, mustard or lemon juice, which have fewer calories.

Fruity summer milkshake

- 1 ripe peach, halved, pitted and chopped
- 150 g (5 oz) strawberries
- 150 g (5 oz) raspberries
- 200 ml (7 fl oz) skimmed milk
- ice cubes

1 Put the peach in a blender or food processor with the strawberries and raspberries and blend to a smooth purée, scraping the mixture down from the sides of the bowl if necessary.

2 Add the milk and blend the ingredients again until the mixture is smooth and frothy. Pour the milkshake over the ice cubes in 2 tall glasses.

Top tip

It's possible to confuse hunger with thirst so, when you feel hungry, try drinking a large glass of water. To stay healthy and hydrated throughout the day it is important to drink plenty of water.

Makes 12
Preparation time 15 minutes
Cooking time 20 minutes

Broccoli & spinach eggahs

- 125 g (4 oz) broccoli
- 100 g (3½ oz) baby spinach leaves
- 6 eggs
- 300 ml (½ pint) semi-skimmed milk
- 2 tablespoons grated Parmesan cheese
- large pinch of ground nutmeg
- oil, for greasing
- salt and pepper

1 Cut the broccoli into small florets and thickly slice the stems. Put in a steamer set over a saucepan of boiling water, cover and cook for 3 minutes. Add the spinach and cook for a further 1 minute or until the spinach has just wilted.

2 Beat together the eggs, milk, Parmesan, nutmeg and a little salt and pepper in a jug. Divide the broccoli and spinach among the sections of a lightly oiled 12-hole deep muffin tin, then pour over the egg mixture.

3 Bake in a preheated oven, 190°C (375°F), Gas Mark 5, for about 15 minutes or until lightly browned, well risen and the egg mixture has set. Leave in the tin for 1–2 minutes, then loosen the edges with a knife and turn out. Serve warm.

Makes 12
Preparation time 10 minutes, plus cooling
Cooking time 20–25 minutes

68
CALORIES
PER SERVING

Potato drop scones

- **550 g (1 lb 2 oz) large potatoes, peeled and cut into small chunks**
- **1½ teaspoons baking powder**
- **2 eggs**
- **75 ml (3 fl oz) milk**
- **vegetable oil, for frying**
- **salt and pepper**

1 Cook the potatoes in a large saucepan of lightly salted boiling water for 15 minutes or until completely tender. Drain well, return to the pan and mash until smooth. Leave to cool slightly.

2 Beat in the baking powder, then the eggs, milk and a little salt and pepper, and continue to beat until everything is evenly combined.

3 Heat a little oil in a heavy-based frying pan. Drop heaped dessertspoonfuls of the mixture into the pan, spacing them slightly apart, and fry for 3–4 minutes, turning once, until golden. Transfer to a serving plate and keep warm. Repeat with the remaining potato mixture to make 12 scones. (If grilling the potato scones, place heaped dessertspoonfuls of the mixture on an oiled, foil-lined baking sheet and cook under a preheated grill for 5 minutes, turning once halfway through the cooking time.) Serve warm.

Serves 8
Preparation time 10 minutes, plus chilling

Smoked mackerel & chive pâté

- **200 g (7 oz) smoked mackerel, skinned, boned and flaked**
- **125 g (4 oz) low-fat soft cheese**
- **1 bunch of chives, chopped**
- **1 tablespoon fat-free vinaigrette**
- **1 tablespoon lemon juice**

1 Put the mackerel and cheese in a bowl and mash together well. Add the remaining ingredients and mix well. Alternatively, mix all the ingredients together in a food processor or blender.

2 Spoon the mixture into 8 small individual serving dishes or 1 large serving dish or mould. Cover and chill for at least 2 hours, or up to 4 hours, before serving.

Top tip

Try having an early night if you feel very hungry at the end of a fast day. Then you can go to sleep safe in the knowledge that you can have a hearty breakfast first thing in the morning.

Smoked salmon Thai rolls

- 12 slices of smoked salmon
- 1 cucumber, peeled, deseeded and cut into matchsticks
- 1 long red chilli, deseeded and thinly sliced
- handful each of coriander, mint and Thai basil leaves

Dressing
- 2 tablespoons sweet chilli sauce
- 2 tablespoons clear honey
- 2 tablespoons lime juice
- 1 tablespoon Thai fish sauce

1 Separate the smoked salmon slices and lay them flat on a work surface. Arrange the cucumber, chilli and herbs on the smoked salmon slices, placing an equal mound on each slice.

2 Make the dressing by combining all the ingredients in a screw-top jar, then drizzle over the cucumber, chilli and herb filling.

3 Roll up the salmon slices to enclose the filling and dressing and serve.

55
CALORIES
PER SERVING

Makes 8
Preparation time 5 minutes
Cooking time 4–5 minutes

Lemon grass fish skewers

- 250 g (8 oz) haddock, boned, skinned and cut into small pieces
- ½ tablespoon mint
- 1 tablespoon coriander leaves
- 1 teaspoon Thai red curry paste
- 1 lime leaf, finely chopped, or the rind of 1 lime
- 2 lemon grass stalks, quartered lengthways
- oil, for brushing

1 Place the fish, mint, coriander, curry paste and lime leaf or rind in a blender or food processor and blend for 15–30 seconds until well combined.

2 Divide the mixture into 8 and form each around a lemon grass stalk 'skewer'. Brush with a little oil and cook under a preheated hot grill for 4–5 minutes until cooked through. Serve immediately.

Makes 10
Preparation time 10 minutes, plus marinating
Cooking time 10 minutes

82
CALORIES
PER SERVING

Chicken satay

- **500 g (1 lb) boneless, skinless chicken breast, cut into about 50 cubes**

Marinade
- **25 g (1 oz) smooth peanut butter**
- **125 ml (4 fl oz) soy sauce**
- **125 ml (4 fl oz) lime juice**
- **15 g (½ oz) curry powder**
- **2 garlic cloves, chopped**
- **1 teaspoon hot chilli pepper sauce**

1 Mix together the marinade ingredients in a non-metallic bowl. Add the chicken and coat well. Cover and leave to marinate in the refrigerator for about 12 hours or overnight.

2 When ready to cook, thread about 5 cubes of chicken on to each of 10 skewers. Cook under a preheated hot grill for 5 minutes on each side until cooked through. Serve hot.

Top tip

Plan your fasting days at the beginning of the week. It is a good idea to fast on days when you will be busy as won't have so much time to think about food if you have a long list of things to get through.

88
CALORIES
PER SERVING

Serves 4
Preparation time 15 minutes, plus chilling
Cooking time 25 minutes

Gazpacho

- **750 g (1½ lb) ripe tomatoes**
- **300 ml (½ pint) water**
- **1 large fennel bulb, trimmed and finely sliced**
- **¾ teaspoon coriander seeds**
- **½ teaspoon mixed peppercorns**
- **1 tablespoon extra virgin olive oil**
- **1 large garlic clove, crushed**
- **1 small onion, chopped**
- **1 tablespoon balsamic vinegar**
- **1 tablespoon lemon juice**
- **¾ teaspoon chopped oregano, plus extra leaves to garnish**
- **1 teaspoon tomato purée**
- **1 rounded teaspoon rock salt**
- **finely sliced green olives, to garnish**

1 Put the tomatoes in a large saucepan or heatproof bowl and pour over enough boiling water to cover, then leave for about 1 minute. Drain and skin the tomatoes carefully, then roughly chop the flesh.

2 Put the measurement water and a little salt in a saucepan and bring to the boil. Add the fennel, cover and simmer for 10 minutes.

3 Meanwhile, crush the coriander seeds and peppercorns using a pestle and mortar. Heat the oil in a large pan, add the crushed spices, garlic and onion and cook gently for 5 minutes.

4 Add the vinegar, lemon juice, tomatoes and chopped oregano. Stir well, then add the fennel with its cooking fluid, the tomato purée and rock salt. Bring to a simmer and cook for 10 minutes. Transfer the mixture to a food processor or blender and whiz together.

5 Cool the gazpacho, then cover and chill for at least several hours or preferably overnight. Serve garnished with oregano leaves and sliced olives.

Serves 4
Preparation time 10 minutes
Cooking time 2 minutes

99
CALORIES
PER SERVING

Watermelon & feta salad

- **1 tablespoon black sesame seeds**
- **500 g (1 lb) watermelon, peeled, deseeded and diced**
- **175 g (6 oz) feta cheese, diced**
- **2½ handfuls of rocket**
- **handful of mint leaves**

Dressing
- **2 tablespoons olive oil**
- **juice of ½ large lemon**
- **salt and pepper**

1 Dry-fry the sesame seeds in a small, nonstick frying pan for a few minutes until aromatic, then set aside.

2 Arrange the watermelon and feta on a large serving plate with the rocket and mint.

3 Make the dressing by combining all the ingredients in a screw-top jar. Drizzle over the salad, scatter over the toasted sesame seeds and serve.

Top tip

Make a list of the reasons why you are fasting and stick it on front of your fridge. This will remind you of your goals whenever you reach for something to eat!

99
CALORIES
PER SERVING

Serves 4
Preparation time 10 minutes, plus cooling
Cooking time 10 minutes

Warm aubergine salad

- 2 tablespoons olive oil
- 2 aubergines, cut into small cubes
- 1 red onion, finely sliced
- 2 tablespoons capers, drained and roughly chopped
- 4 tomatoes, chopped
- 4 tablespoons chopped parsley
- 1 tablespoon balsamic vinegar
- salt and pepper

1 Heat the oil in a nonstick frying pan, add the aubergines and fry for 10 minutes until golden and softened.

2 Add the onion, capers, tomatoes, parsley and vinegar and stir to combine. Season lightly with salt and pepper. Remove from the heat and leave to cool for 10 minutes before serving.

Serves 4
Preparation time 10 minutes
Cooking time 10 minutes

93
CALORIES
PER SERVING

Garlic mushrooms with spinach & crispy bacon

- **8 open-cap mushrooms**
- **4 tablespoons water**
- **200 g (7 oz) extra-light garlic and herb cream cheese**
- **grated rind of 1 lemon**
- **100 g (3½ oz) baby leaf spinach**
- **4 lean back bacon rashers, grilled until crisp, then roughly chopped**
- **salt and pepper**

1 Put the mushrooms, gill sides up, in a large nonstick frying pan with the measurement water.

2 Mix together the cream cheese and lemon rind in a bowl, then season with salt and pepper. Divide the mixture among the mushroom caps. Cover and cook over a low heat for 5–6 minutes.

3 Layer the spinach over the mushrooms, re-cover and cook for a further 2 minutes until the spinach has wilted.

4 Divide the mushrooms among 4 warm serving plates, then top with the bacon and serve.

Serves 4
Preparation time 10 minutes
Cooking time 25 minutes

Mushroom stroganoff

- 1 tablespoon rapeseed oil
- 1 large onion, thinly sliced
- 4 celery sticks, thinly sliced
- 2 garlic cloves, crushed
- 600 g (1¼ lb) mixed mushrooms, roughly chopped
- 2 teaspoons smoked paprika
- 250 ml (8 fl oz) vegetable stock
- 150 ml (¼ pint) soured cream
- pepper

1 Heat the oil in a nonstick frying pan, add the onion, celery and garlic and cook for 5 minutes or until beginning to soften. Add the mushrooms and paprika and cook for a further 5 minutes.

2 Pour in the stock and cook for a further 10 minutes or until the liquid is reduced by half.

3 Stir in the soured cream and season with pepper. Cook over a medium heat for 5 minutes. Serve immediately.

Serves 4
Preparation time 15 minutes
Cooking time 25–30 minutes

44 CALORIES PER SERVING

Ratatouille

- 2 large beef tomatoes
- ½ tablespoon olive oil
- 375 g (12 oz) aubergines, cut into 1 cm (½ inch) chunks
- ½ large Spanish onion, cut into 1 cm (½ inch) chunks
- 2 celery sticks, roughly chopped
- ½ teaspoon chopped basil

1 Put the tomatoes in a large saucepan or heatproof bowl and pour over enough boiling water to cover, then leave for about 1 minute. Drain, skin the tomatoes carefully, deseed and roughly chop the flesh.

2 Heat the oil in a nonstick frying pan until very hot, add the aubergines and fry for about 10–15 minutes until very soft.

3 Meanwhile, put the onion and celery in a saucepan with a little water and cook for 3–5 minutes until tender but still firm. Add the tomatoes and basil, then add the aubergine. Cook for 15 minutes, stirring occasionally. Serve hot.

Serves 4
Preparation time 10 minutes
Cooking time 15–20 minutes

Mushroom & pea bhaji

- 2 tablespoons vegetable oil
- 50 g (2 oz) onion, finely sliced
- ¼ teaspoon cumin seeds, crushed
- ¼ teaspoon mustard seeds
- 125 g (4 oz) tomatoes, chopped
- 1 green chilli, deseeded and finely chopped
- 425 g (14 oz) button mushrooms, halved (or quartered if larger)
- 150 g (5 oz) frozen peas
- ½ teaspoon chilli powder
- ¼ teaspoon ground turmeric
- 1 red pepper, cored, deseeded and chopped
- 4 garlic cloves, crushed
- 2 tablespoons coriander leaves
- chopped spring onions or chives, to garnish

1 Heat the oil in a saucepan, add the onion and fry gently for 2–3 minutes until beginning to soften. Add the cumin and mustard seeds and fry, stirring, for a further 2 minutes.

2 Add the tomatoes, chilli, mushrooms and peas. Stir and cook for 2 minutes.

3 Add the chilli powder and turmeric and mix well, then cook, uncovered, for a further 5–7 minutes.

4 Add the red pepper, garlic and coriander and cook for 5 minutes until the mixture is quite dry. Serve garnished with the spring onions or chives.

100
CALORIES
PER SERVING

Red fruit salad

- **250 g (8 oz) fresh strawberries**
- **250 g (8 oz) fresh raspberries**
- **250 g (8 oz) seedless red grapes**
- **250 g (8 oz) watermelon, cubed**
- **1 tablespoon balsamic vinegar**
- **50 ml (2 fl oz) port**

1 Add the fruit to a bowl and mix, add the vinegar and port and mix again.

2 Chill the fruit for 10–20 minutes before serving.

Top tip

Try drinking green tea. It contains no calories, is rich in antioxidants and may even marginally increase your metabolic rate, giving you a slight weight loss advantage.

Serves 8
Preparation time 5 minutes, plus chilling

Mango & lychee mousse

- 400 g (13 oz) can mango slices in juice
- 400 g (13 oz) can lychees
- 2 tablespoons low-fat natural yogurt
- 4 tablespoons fromage frais
- 1 teaspoon lime juice
- 1 tablespoon skimmed-milk powder
- ½ teaspoon vanilla essence
- 2 teaspoons clear honey
- pared rind from unwaxed orange and lime, to decorate

1 Place all the ingredients except the pared rind in a blender or food processor and blend together. If you prefer a thicker consistency, add 1 extra tablespoon of skimmed-milk powder.

2 Divide the mixture among 8 dessert glasses and chill for at least 30 minutes.

3 Decorate with a little pared orange and lime rind and serve.

Makes 30
Preparation time 10 minutes
Cooking time 5–6 minutes

30
CALORIES
PER SERVING

Cranberry & hazelnut cookies

- 50 g (2 oz) unsalted butter, softened
- 40 g (1½ oz) granulated sugar
- 25 g (1 oz) soft light brown sugar
- 1 egg, beaten
- a few drops of vanilla essence
- 150 g (5 oz) self-raising flour, sifted
- 50 g (2 oz) rolled oats
- 50 g (2 oz) dried cranberries
- 40 g (1½ oz) hazelnuts, toasted and chopped

1 Beat together the butter, sugars, egg and vanilla essence in a large bowl until smooth. Stir in the flour and oats, then the dried cranberries and chopped hazelnuts.

2 Place teaspoonfuls of the mixture on baking sheets lined with greaseproof paper or nonstick baking paper and flatten them slightly with the back of a fork.

3 Bake in a preheated oven, 180°C (350°F), Gas Mark 4, for about 5–6 minutes until browned. Transfer to a wire rack and leave to cool. Store in an airtight container for up to 5 days.

Serves 6
Preparation time 10 minutes
Cooking time 7–8 minutes

Minted zabaglione with blueberries

- 4 egg yolks
- 3 tablespoons light cane sugar
- 125 ml (4 fl oz) sweet white wine or sherry
- 150 g (5 oz) blueberries, plus extra to decorate
- 4 teaspoons chopped mint, plus extra to decorate

1 Put the egg yolks and sugar in a large bowl set over a saucepan of simmering water. Use a hand-held electric whisk or a balloon whisk to beat the yolks and sugar for 2–3 minutes until they are thick and pale.

2 Whisk in the white wine or sherry, little by little, and continue whisking for about 5 minutes until the mixture is light, thick and foaming.

3 Warm the blueberries in a small saucepan with 1 tablespoon of water and spoon them into the bases of 6 small glasses. Whisk the mint into the foaming wine mixture and pour it over the blueberries. Stand the glasses on small plates or on a tray and arrange a few extra berries around them. Top with a little chopped mint and serve immediately.

200
CALORIES
AND UNDER

Serves 2
Preparation time 10 minutes
Cooking time 25–35 minutes

Moroccan baked eggs

- ½ tablespoon olive oil
- ½ onion, chopped
- 1 garlic clove, sliced
- ½ teaspoon ras el hanout
- pinch of ground cinnamon
- ½ teaspoon ground coriander
- 400 g (13 oz) cherry tomatoes
- 2 tablespoons chopped coriander
- 2 eggs
- salt and pepper

1 Heat the oil in a frying pan, add the onion and garlic and cook for 6–7 minutes until softened and lightly golden. Stir in the spices and cook, stirring, for a further 1 minute.

2 Add the tomatoes and season well with salt and pepper, then simmer gently for 8–10 minutes.

3 Scatter over 1 tablespoon of the coriander, then divide the tomato mixture between 2 individual ovenproof dishes. Break an egg into each dish.

4 Bake in a preheated oven, 220°C (425°F), Gas Mark 7, for 8–10 minutes until the egg whites are set but the yolks are still slightly runny. Cook for a further 2–3 minutes if you prefer the eggs to be cooked through. Serve scattered with the remaining coriander.

Serves 4
Preparation time 15 minutes
Cooking time 35 minutes

155
CALORIES
PER SERVING

Fennel & white bean soup

- **900 ml (1½ pints) vegetable stock**
- **2 fennel bulbs, trimmed and chopped**
- **1 onion, chopped**
- **1 courgette, chopped**
- **1 carrot, chopped**
- **2 garlic cloves, finely sliced**
- **6 tomatoes, finely chopped, or 400 g (13 oz) can tomatoes**
- **2 × 400 g (13 oz) cans butter beans, rinsed and drained**
- **2 tablespoons chopped sage**
- **pepper**

1 Pour 300 ml (½ pint) of the stock into a large saucepan. Add the fennel, onion, courgette, carrot and garlic, cover and bring to the boil. Boil for 5 minutes, then remove the lid, reduce the heat and simmer gently for about 20 minutes until the vegetables are tender.

2 Stir in the tomatoes, beans and sage. Season with pepper and pour in the remaining stock. Simmer for 5 minutes, then leave to cool slightly.

3 Transfer 300 ml (½ pint) of the soup to a blender or food processor and blend until smooth. Return the blended soup to the pan, stir to combine with the unblended soup and heat through gently before serving.

160
CALORIES
PER SERVING

Serves 4
Preparation time 15 minutes
Cooking time 25 minutes

Sweet potato & cabbage soup

- 2 onions, chopped
- 2 garlic cloves, sliced
- 4 lean back bacon rashers, chopped
- 500 g (1 lb) sweet potatoes, peeled and chopped
- 2 parsnips, peeled and chopped
- 1 teaspoon chopped thyme
- 900 ml (1½ pints) vegetable stock
- 1 baby Savoy cabbage, shredded

1 Put the onions, garlic and bacon in a large saucepan and fry for 2–3 minutes. Add the sweet potatoes, parsnips, thyme and stock and bring to the boil, then reduce the heat and simmer for 15 minutes.

2 Transfer two-thirds of the soup to a blender or food processor and blend until smooth. Return the blended soup to the pan, add the cabbage and simmer for a further 5–7 minutes until the cabbage is just cooked.

Serves 4
Preparation time 5 minutes
Cooking time 20–25 minutes

160
CALORIES
PER SERVING

Onion & fennel soup

- 1 tablespoon olive oil
- 6 onions, chopped
- 2 tablespoons chopped thyme
- 1 tablespoon rosemary leaves
- 1.2 litres (2 pints) vegetable or beef stock
- 600 ml (1 pint) water
- 425 g (14 oz) trimmed fennel, finely sliced
- salt and pepper
- Parmesan cheese shavings, to garnish

1 Heat the oil in a large saucepan over a low heat, add the onions, thyme and rosemary and cook for 10 minutes.

2 Add the stock, measurement water and fennel and cook over a medium heat for 10–15 minutes, or until the fennel is tender. Season with salt.

3 Serve the soup sprinkled with pepper and garnished with Parmesan shavings.

Top tip

Soup is a great, low-calorie option when you want a filling lunch. Cook a big batch of soup in advance and freeze it in portions to defrost for a quick and easy lunch.

200 CALORIES PER SERVING

Serves 4
Preparation time 10 minutes, plus standing

Moroccan tomato & chickpea salad

- 1 red onion, finely sliced
- 2 × 400 g (13 oz) cans chickpeas, rinsed and drained
- 4 tomatoes, chopped
- 4 tablespoons lemon juice
- 1 tablespoon olive oil
- handful of fresh mixed herbs, such as mint and parsley, chopped
- pinch of paprika
- pinch of ground cumin
- salt and pepper

1 Mix together all the ingredients in a large non-metallic bowl and leave to stand for 10 minutes to allow the flavours to infuse before serving.

Top tip

If you can't resist a taste of sweetness on your fast day, the best option would be to choose an airy dessert, like a mousse, or a dish that uses fresh or dried fruit to provide the sweetness.

Tabbouleh salad

- **175 g (6 oz) bulgar wheat**
- **300 ml (½ pint) boiling water**
- **1 red onion, finely chopped**
- **3 tomatoes, diced**
- **½ cucumber, chopped**
- **10 tablespoons chopped parsley**
- **5 tablespoons chopped mint**

Dressing
- **100 ml (3½ fl oz) lemon juice**
- **2 teaspoons olive oil**
- **pepper**

1 Put the bulgar wheat in a bowl. Pour over the boiling water and leave to stand for 30 minutes, or according to the packet instructions, until the grains swell and soften.

2 Drain the bulgar wheat and press to remove the excess moisture. Put the bulgar wheat in a salad bowl with the onion, tomatoes, cucumber, parsley and mint and toss to combine.

3 Make the dressing by combining all the ingredients in a screw-top jar. Pour over the salad, toss well and serve.

Serves 6
Preparation time 15 minutes, plus standing
Cooking time 5 minutes

Orange & almond couscous salad

- 250 ml (8 fl oz) apple juice
- 175 g (6 oz) couscous
- ½ red pepper, cored, deseeded and diced
- 4 tablespoons chopped parsley
- 3 tablespoons chopped mint
- 25 g (1 oz) currants
- 2 oranges
- 1 red onion, sliced
- 25 g (1 oz) flaked almonds

Dressing
- juice of 1 orange
- juice of 1 lemon or lime
- 2 teaspoons olive or hazelnut oil
- 1 teaspoon honey

1 Pour the apple juice into a saucepan and bring to the boil, then slowly stir in the couscous. Remove the pan from heat, cover and leave to stand for 10 minutes. Fluff up with a fork.

2 Add the red pepper, herbs and currants to the couscous and toss to combine. Transfer to a serving bowl.

3 Cut the top and bottom off the oranges with a serrated knife to reveal the flesh, then cut away the remaining peel and pith. Holding the fruit above the serving bowl, cut between the membranes to release the fruit segments over the couscous, then scatter over the onion.

4 To make the dressing, put all the ingredients in a small saucepan and heat gently to dissolve the honey – do not allow to boil. Drizzle over the salad and serve scattered with the almonds.

Serves 4
Preparation time 15 minutes, plus marinating
Cooking time 1 minute

178
CALORIES
PER SERVING

Asian tuna salad

- 350 g (12 oz) tuna steak, cut into strips
- 3 tablespoons soy sauce
- 1 teaspoon wasabi paste
- 1 tablespoon sake or dry white wine
- 200 g (7 oz) mixed salad leaves
- 150 g (5 oz) baby yellow tomatoes, halved
- 1 cucumber, sliced into wide, fine strips

Dressing
- 2 tablespoons soy sauce
- 1 tablespoon lime juice
- 1 teaspoon brown sugar
- 2 teaspoons sesame oil

1 Mix together the tuna, soy sauce, wasabi and sake or white wine in a non-metallic bowl. Leave to marinate for 10 minutes.

2 Arrange the salad leaves, tomatoes and cucumber on 4 serving plates.

3 Make the dressing by combining all the ingredients in a screw-top jar.

4 Heat a nonstick frying pan over a high heat, add the tuna and fry for about 10 seconds on each side or until seared. Place the tuna on top of the salad, drizzle with the dressing and serve.

Serves 4
Preparation time 10 minutes, plus chilling
Cooking time 15–20 minutes

Chicken salad Thai style

- 150 g (5 oz) cooked chicken breast, shredded
- 3 tablespoons coriander leaves
- 150 g (5 oz) pak choi, shredded

Dressing
- 1 tablespoon groundnut oil
- 1 tablespoon Thai fish sauce
- juice of 1 lime
- juice of 1 small orange
- 1 garlic clove, crushed
- 3 tablespoons roughly chopped basil
- pepper

To garnish
- 2 spring onions, green stems only, shredded lengthways
- 1 plump red chilli, deseeded and sliced diagonally

1 Make the dressing by combining all the ingredients in a screw-top jar.

2 Mix together the chicken and coriander leaves in a bowl, then stir in the dressing.

3 Line a serving dish with the pak choi, spoon the dressed chicken on top, cover and chill before serving. Serve garnished with spring onion shreds and red chilli slices.

Serves 4
Preparation time 5 minutes, plus soaking
Cooking time 4–5 minutes

Hot chicken liver salad

- 400 g (13 oz) chicken livers, trimmed and halved
- 60 ml (2½ fl oz) milk
- 2 teaspoons chopped thyme
- 1 tablespoon olive oil
- 2 garlic cloves, crushed
- 1 red chilli, thinly sliced (optional)
- 200 g (7 oz) can water chestnuts, drained and halved

To serve
- 200 g (7 oz) chicory, leaves separated
- 1½–2 tablespoons balsamic vinegar

1 Soak the chicken livers in the milk for 30 minutes to remove any bitterness. Discard the milk and pat the livers dry with kitchen paper. Sprinkle the thyme over both sides of the livers.

2 Heat the oil in a large frying pan, add the garlic and chilli, if using, and soften for 30 seconds. Add the chicken livers and water chestnuts and cook over a medium heat for 3–4 minutes until the livers are browned on the outside but still pink in the centre.

3 Serve on a bed of crispy raw chicory, drizzled with balsamic vinegar and any remaining pan juices.

Serves 4
Preparation time 10 minutes

Caprese salad

- 500 g (1 lb) beef tomatoes, sliced
- 2 balls of mozzarella cheese, sliced
- 3 tablespoons vinaigrette
- 2 tablespoons chopped basil
- salt and pepper

1 Arrange the tomato and mozzarella in overlapping slices on a large serving plate.

2 Drizzle with the vinaigrette.

3 Scatter with the basil, season with salt and pepper and serve.

Top tip

Keep a record of everything you eat and drink in a food journal. This is a good way to make sure that you are staying within you calorie limit while still eating a balanced diet.

Serves 4
Preparation time 15 minutes, plus marinating
Cooking time 10 minutes

195 CALORIES PER SERVING

Thai-style fish kebabs

- 500–750 g (1–1½ lb) firm white fish, such as monkfish, swordfish, cod or haddock, cut into large cubes
- 1 courgette, cut into 8 pieces
- 1 onion, quartered and layers separated
- 8 mushrooms
- vegetable oil, for brushing

Marinade
- grated rind and juice of 2 limes
- 1 garlic clove, finely chopped
- 2 tablespoons finely sliced fresh root ginger
- 2 chillies, deseeded and finely chopped
- 2 lemon grass stalks, finely chopped
- handful of coriander leaves, finely chopped
- 1 glass of red wine
- 2 tablespoons sesame oil
- pepper

1 Mix together the marinade ingredients in a large non-metallic bowl. Add the fish, courgette, onion and mushrooms and coat well. Cover and leave to marinate in the refrigerator for 1 hour.

2 Brush the rack of a grill pan lightly with oil to prevent the kebabs from sticking. Thread 4 skewers alternately with the chunks of fish, mushrooms, courgette and onion. Brush with a little oil and cook under a preheated hot grill for about 10 minutes, turning the skewers frequently, until cooked through. Serve hot.

199
CALORIES
PER SERVING

Serves 4
Preparation time 15 minutes, plus standing
Cooking time 5 minutes

Crab & noodle Asian wraps

- 200 g (7 oz) rice noodles
- 1 bunch of spring onions, finely sliced
- 1.5 cm (¾ inch) piece of fresh root ginger, peeled and grated
- 1 garlic clove, finely sliced
- 1 red chilli, finely chopped
- 2 tablespoons chopped coriander
- 1 tablespoon chopped mint
- ¼ cucumber, cut into fine matchsticks
- 2 × 175 g (6 oz) cans crabmeat, drained, or 300 g (10 oz) fresh white crabmeat
- 1 tablespoon sesame oil
- 1 tablespoon sweet chilli sauce
- 1 teaspoon Thai fish sauce
- 16 Chinese pancakes or Vietnamese ricepaper wrappers

1 Cook the rice noodles according to the packet instructions. Drain, then refresh under cold running water.

2 Mix together all the remaining ingredients, except the pancakes or ricepaper wrappers, in a large bowl. Add the noodles and toss to mix. Cover and leave to stand for 10 minutes to allow the flavours to develop, then transfer to a serving dish.

3 Allowing 4 per person, top the pancakes or ricepaper wrappers with some of the crab and noodle mixture and roll up to eat.

Serves 6
Preparation time 25–30 minutes
Cooking time 10 minutes

185
CALORIES
PER SERVING

Crab & coriander cakes

- **375 g (12 oz) canned crabmeat, drained**
- **250 g (8 oz) cold mashed potatoes**
- **2 tablespoons chopped coriander**
- **1 bunch of spring onions, finely sliced**
- **grated rind and juice of ½ lemon**
- **2 eggs, beaten**
- **flour, for coating**
- **150 g (5 oz) fresh white breadcrumbs**
- **1 tablespoon vegetable oil**

1 Mix together the crabmeat, mashed potatoes, coriander, spring onions, lemon rind and juice in a large bowl, then add half the beaten egg to bind.

2 Form the mixture into 12 cakes about 1 cm (½ inch) thick. Coat the cakes with flour, then dip into the remaining egg and then the breadcrumbs.

3 Heat the oil in a nonstick frying pan, add the cakes and fry for about 10 minutes until golden, turning once or twice. Remove from the pan and drain on kitchen paper. Divide the crab cakes among 6 serving plates and serve hot.

Serves 4
Preparation time 30 minutes, plus marinating
Cooking time 3–5 minutes

Marinated prawns & courgette ribbons

- 450 g (14½ oz) courgettes, sliced into fine ribbons with a vegetable peeler
- 28 large raw prawns, peeled but with tails still intact, heads removed
- chopped flat-leaf parsley, to garnish

Marinade
- large pinch of saffron threads
- 8 tablespoons lemon juice
- 6 garlic cloves, roughly chopped
- 2 tablespoons rice wine vinegar
- 4 tablespoons olive oil
- 2 tablespoons capers, drained

1 Mix together all the marinade ingredients, lightly crushing the capers against the side of the bowl. Spoon two-thirds of the marinade mixture on top of the courgette ribbons in a large non-metallic bowl. Cover and leave to marinate in the refrigerator for 3–4 hours.

2 Meanwhile, prepare the prawns. Hold the tail underside up and cut each prawn in half lengthways. Pull out any black intestinal thread, rinse, pat dry on kitchen paper and place in a shallow non-metallic dish. Alternatively, ask your fishmonger to prepare the prawns for you. Pour the remaining marinade over the prawns, cover and leave to marinate in the refrigerator for 3–4 hours.

3 When ready to cook, put the courgettes in a large frying pan with their marinade and simmer over a medium-low heat for 3–5 minutes.

4 Meanwhile, cook the prawns under a preheated grill for 3–4 minutes until pink and sizzling, basting with the marinade. Do not overcook them.

5 Pile the courgettes in the centre of a warm serving dish, top with the prawns and serve garnished with chopped parsley.

Serves 4
Preparation time 10 minutes
Cooking time 10 minutes

182
CALORIES
PER SERVING

Pan-fried plaice with mustard sauce

- 1 teaspoon olive oil
- 1 small onion, finely chopped
- 1 garlic clove, crushed
- 4 plaice or sole fillets, about 150 g (5 oz) each
- 125 ml (4 fl oz) dry white wine
- 2 tablespoons wholegrain mustard
- 200 g (7 oz) crème fraîche
- 2 tablespoons chopped fresh mixed herbs

1 Heat the oil in a large frying pan, add the onion and garlic and fry for 3 minutes until softened.

2 Add the fish fillets and cook for 1 minute on each side, then add the wine and simmer until reduced by half.

3 Stir through the remaining ingredients and bring to the boil, then reduce the heat and simmer for 3–4 minutes until the sauce has thickened slightly and the fish is tender. Serve immediately.

Top tip

Reward yourself for your successes. Set yourself targets and, once you have reached them, treat yourself to something nice.

Serves 6
Preparation time 10 minutes, plus chilling (optional)
Cooking time 5 minutes

Parsley & garlic sardines

- 12 fresh sardines, cleaned, or use fillets if preferred

Marinade
- 50 g (2 oz) chopped parsley
- 1 teaspoon ground black pepper
- 1 garlic clove, crushed
- finely grated rind and juice of 1 lemon
- 2 tablespoons white wine
- 1 tablespoon olive oil

1 Put all the marinade ingredients in a small saucepan and bring to the boil, then remove from the heat.

2 Place the sardines on a hot barbecue or on a preheated hot griddle or under a hot grill. Cook for 1–2 minutes on each side until crisp and golden.

3 Arrange the sardines in a single layer in a shallow serving dish. Pour the warm marinade over the sardines and serve hot. Alternatively, cover and chill for at least 1 hour before serving cold.

Serves 4
Preparation time 15 minutes, plus chilling
Cooking time 6–8 minutes

135
CALORIES
PER SERVING

Chicken burgers with tomato salsa

- 1 garlic clove, crushed
- 3 spring onions, finely sliced
- 1 tablespoon pesto
- 2 tablespoons chopped fresh mixed herbs, such as parsley, tarragon and thyme
- 375 g (12 oz) minced chicken
- 2 sun-dried tomatoes, finely chopped
- 1 teaspoon olive oil

Tomato salsa
- 250 g (8 oz) cherry tomatoes, quartered
- 1 red chilli, deseeded and finely chopped
- 1 tablespoon chopped coriander
- grated rind and juice of 1 lime

1 Mix together all the ingredients for the burgers except the oil. Divide the mixture into 4 and form neat, flattened rounds. Cover and chill for 30 minutes.

2 Meanwhile, mix together all the tomato salsa ingredients in a bowl.

3 Lightly brush the burgers with the oil and cook under a preheated hot grill or on a barbecue for 3–4 minutes on each side until cooked through. Serve immediately with the salsa.

Makes 16
Preparation time 5 minutes, plus marinating
Cooking time 50 minutes

Sticky chicken drumsticks

- 16 chicken drumsticks
- 4 tablespoons honey
- finely grated rind and juice of 1 lemon
- finely grated rind and juice of 1 orange
- 3 tablespoons Worcestershire sauce
- 4 tablespoons tomato ketchup

1 Make several diagonal cuts through the fleshy part of each chicken drumstick and arrange in a single layer in a shallow ovenproof dish.

2 Mix together the remaining ingredients and spoon over the chicken. Cover and leave to marinate in the refrigerator until ready to cook.

3 Bake in a preheated oven, 180°C (350°F), Gas Mark 4, for about 50 minutes, turning and basting frequently until the chicken is cooked through and thickly coated with the sticky glaze. Serve hot or chill thoroughly and serve cold.

Serves 4
Preparation time 10 minutes, plus marinating
Cooking time 2–3 minutes

140
CALORIES
PER SERVING

Beef skewers with dipping sauce

- **350 g (11½ oz) lean rump steak, cut into strips**

Marinade
- **1 tablespoon sweet chilli sauce**
- **½ teaspoon cumin seeds, toasted (see page 61)**
- **½ teaspoon ground coriander**
- **1 teaspoon olive oil**

Dipping sauce
- **1 tablespoon sweet chilli sauce**
- **1 teaspoon Thai fish sauce**
- **1 teaspoon white wine vinegar**

To garnish
- **2 tablespoons chopped coriander**
- **1 tablespoon unsalted peanuts, roughly chopped (optional)**

1 Mix together the marinade ingredients in a non-metallic bowl. Add the steak and stir well to coat, then cover and leave to marinate in the refrigerator for 30 minutes.

2 Thread the steak on to 4 bamboo skewers that have been soaked in water for at least 20 minutes. Cook on a hot griddle or under a preheated hot grill for 2–3 minutes until cooked through.

3 Meanwhile, mix together the sauce ingredients in a small serving bowl. Serve the skewers with the dipping sauce, scattered with the chopped coriander and peanuts, if liked.

Serves 6
Preparation time 20 minutes
Cooking time 25 minutes

Piperade with sofrito and pastrami

- 6 large eggs
- thyme sprigs, leaves removed, or large pinch of dried thyme, plus extra sprigs to garnish
- 1 tablespoon olive oil
- 125 g (4 oz) pastrami, thinly sliced
- salt and pepper

Sofrito
- 375 g (12 oz), or 3 small, different coloured peppers
- 500 g (1 lb) tomatoes
- 1 tablespoon olive oil
- 1 onion, finely chopped
- 2 garlic cloves, crushed

1 To make the sofrito, grill or cook the peppers directly in a gas flame for about 10 minutes, turning them until the skins have blistered and blackened. Rub the skins from the flesh and discard. Rinse the peppers under cold running water. Halve and deseed, then cut the flesh into strips.

2 Put the tomatoes in a large saucepan or heatproof bowl and pour over enough boiling water to cover, then leave for about 1 minute. Drain, skin the tomatoes carefully and then chop the flesh.

3 Heat the oil in a large frying pan, add the onion and cook gently for 10 minutes until softened and transparent. Add the garlic, tomatoes and peppers and simmer for 5 minutes until any juice has evaporated from the tomatoes. Set aside until ready to serve.

4 Beat together the eggs, thyme and salt and pepper in a bowl. Heat the oil in a saucepan, add the eggs, stirring until they are lightly scrambled.

5 Meanwhile, reheat the sofrito. Stir the scrambled eggs into the reheated sofrito and spoon on to 6 serving plates. Arrange slices of pastrami around the eggs and serve immediately, garnished with sprigs of thyme.

Serves 4
Preparation time 5 minutes
Cooking time 5–7 minutes

195
CALORIES
PER SERVING

Calves' liver with Marsala sauce

- 1 tablespoon rice flour
- 500 g (1 lb) calves' liver, thinly sliced
- 1 tablespoon olive oil
- 25 g (1 oz) butter
- 1 garlic clove, chopped
- 2 teaspoons chopped sage, plus extra sprigs to garnish
- 125 ml (4 fl oz) chicken stock
- 3 tablespoons Marsala
- salt and pepper

1 Place the flour on a plate and season with salt and pepper, then coat the liver in the flour.

2 Heat the oil and butter in a large frying pan, add the garlic and liver and fry for 1–2 minutes on each side. Add the chopped sage and stock and cook for a further 2 minutes. Remove the liver from the pan with a slotted spoon and keep warm on a serving dish.

3 Add the Marsala to the pan and season with salt and pepper. Bring the sauce to the boil, stirring continuously for 1 minute, then pour over the liver and serve immediately, garnished with sprigs of sage.

155
CALORIES
PER SERVING

Serves 4
Preparation time 5 minutes
Cooking time 13 minutes

Green beans with ham & garlic

- **500 g (1 lb) green beans, trimmed**
- **2 tablespoons olive oil**
- **1 onion, sliced**
- **1 garlic clove, crushed**
- **75 g (3 oz) piece of Parma ham, cubed**
- **salt and pepper**

1 Cook the beans in a saucepan of salted boiling water for about 8 minutes until almost tender.

2 Meanwhile, heat the oil in a frying pan, add the onion and fry until softened. Add the garlic and ham and cook for 1 minute.

3 Drain the beans and add to the frying pan, then cover and cook for 5 minutes. Season with salt and pepper and serve.

Top tip

Find yourself a diet buddy. Dieting together can introduce a bit of healthy competition and you can encourage each other when the going gets tough.

Serves 2
Preparation time 10 minutes
Cooking time 25 minutes

168
CALORIES
PER SERVING

Mushroom & artichoke bake

- **500 g (1 lb) canned artichoke hearts, drained**
- **1 teaspoon olive oil, plus extra for greasing**
- **50 g (2 oz) onion, finely chopped**
- **2 garlic cloves, finely chopped**
- **300 g (10 oz) mushrooms, sliced**
- **1 tablespoon chopped basil**
- **1 tablespoon chopped oregano**
- **1 tablespoon lemon juice**
- **1 tablespoon dry white wine**
- **1 tablespoon brown breadcrumbs**
- **1 tablespoon grated Parmesan cheese**
- **salt and pepper**
- **parsley sprigs, to garnish**

1 Place the artichokes in a lightly oiled, medium-sized baking tin.

2 Heat the oil in a medium, nonstick frying pan over a medium heat, add the onion and garlic and fry gently, stirring frequently, for 3 minutes. Stir in the mushrooms and herbs.

3 Add the lemon juice and wine, then season with salt and pepper and cook for a further 3 minutes. Remove from the heat and stir in the breadcrumbs.

4 Spoon the mushroom mixture evenly over the artichokes, then bake in a preheated oven, 180°C (350°F), Gas Mark 4, for 10 minutes.

5 Remove from the oven and sprinkle over the Parmesan. Bake for a further 10 minutes, then serve garnished with sprigs of parsley.

199
CALORIES
PER SERVING

Serves 4
Preparation time 10 minutes
Cooking time 20–25 minutes

Baked vegetable frittata

- 250 g (8 oz) asparagus, trimmed and halved
- 1 tablespoon extra virgin olive oil
- 2 leeks, trimmed and sliced
- 2 garlic cloves, crushed
- 2 tablespoons chopped basil
- 6 eggs
- 2 tablespoons milk
- butter, for greasing
- 2 tablespoons grated Parmesan cheese
- salt and pepper

1 Cook the asparagus in a saucepan of lightly salted boiling water for 2 minutes, drain and shake dry.

2 Meanwhile, heat the oil in a large frying pan, add the leeks and garlic and fry gently for 5 minutes or until softened. Add the asparagus and basil and remove the pan from the heat.

3 Beat together the eggs and milk in a bowl and season with salt and pepper. Stir in the vegetable mixture and pour into a greased 1.2 litre (2 pint) ovenproof dish.

4 Scatter over the Parmesan and bake in a preheated oven, 200°C (400°F), Gas Mark 6, for 15–20 minutes until firm in the centre. Serve immediately.

Serves 6
Preparation time 10 minutes
Cooking time 30–35 minutes

200 CALORIES PER SERVING

Courgette & mint frittatas with tomato sauce

- 1 tablespoon olive oil, plus extra for greasing
- 1 onion, finely chopped
- 2 courgettes, about 375 g (12 oz) in total, halved lengthways and thinly sliced
- 6 eggs
- 300 ml (½ pint) milk
- 3 tablespoons grated Parmesan cheese
- 2 tablespoons chopped mint, plus extra leaves to garnish (optional)
- salt and pepper

Tomato sauce
- 1 tablespoon olive oil
- 1 onion, finely chopped
- 1–2 garlic cloves, crushed (optional)
- 500 g (1 lb) plum tomatoes, chopped

1 To make the sauce, heat the oil in a saucepan, add the onion and fry for 5 minutes, stirring occasionally until softened and just beginning to brown. Add the garlic, if using, and tomatoes and season with salt and pepper. Stir and simmer for 5 minutes until the tomatoes are soft. Transfer to a blender or food processor and blend until smooth, then pass the sauce through a fine sieve into a bowl and keep warm.

2 Heat the oil in a frying pan, add the onion and fry until softened and just beginning to brown. Add the courgettes, stir to combine and cook for 3–4 minutes until softened but not browned.

3 Beat together the eggs, milk, Parmesan and mint in a jug, then stir in the courgettes and season well. Pour the mixture into the sections of a lightly oiled 12-hole deep muffin tin.

4 Bake in a preheated oven, 190°C (375°F), Gas Mark 5, for about 15 minutes until lightly browned, well risen and the egg mixture has set. Leave in the tin for 1–2 minutes, then loosen the edges with a knife and turn out.

5 Place 2 frittatas on each of 6 serving plates. Serve with the warm tomato sauce, garnished with mint leaves, if liked.

176
CALORIES
PER SERVING

Serves 4
Preparation time 30 minutes
Cooking time 12 minutes

Vietnamese vegetable spring rolls with plum sauce

- 200 g (7 oz) pak choi
- 2 tablespoons sunflower oil
- 100 g (3½ oz) sweet potato, peeled and cut into matchstick strips
- 100 g (3½ oz) carrot, cut into matchstick strips
- ½ bunch of spring onions, cut into matchstick strips
- 50 g (2 oz) bean sprouts,
- 2 garlic cloves, finely chopped
- 2 cm (¾ inch) piece of fresh root ginger, peeled and finely chopped
- 50 g (2 oz), or 8, rice pancakes
- bunch of coriander

Plum sauce
- 4 ripe red plums, about 250 g (8 oz) in total, stoned and chopped
- 2 tablespoons water
- 1 tablespoon soy sauce
- 1 tablespoon caster sugar
- made-up wasabi, to taste

1 Cut the leaves from the pak choi and slice the stems into matchstick strips. Heat 1 tablespoon of the oil in a wok or large frying pan, add the sweet potato and carrot and stir-fry for 2 minutes. Add the spring onions and pak choi stems and cook for 1 minute. Mix in the bean sprouts, garlic and ginger and cook for 1 minute. Transfer to a bowl.

2 Heat the remaining oil in the pan, add the pak choi leaves and cook for 2–3 minutes until just wilted.

3 Dip a rice pancake into a bowl of hot water and leave for 20–30 seconds until softened. Lift out and place on a clean tea towel. Top with a pak choi leaf, one-eighth of the vegetable mixture and 2 stems of coriander. Fold in the pancake edges and roll up tightly. Repeat with the remaining pancakes to make 8 spring rolls. Cover with clingfilm and set aside. Serve within 1 hour.

4 Meanwhile, make the sauce. Put the plums in a small saucepan with the measurement water, cover and cook for 5 minutes until softened. Purée the plums with the soy sauce in a food processor, then mix in the sugar and wasabi to taste.

5 Garnish the spring rolls with the remaining sprigs of coriander and serve 2 per person with small bowls of the sauce.

Serves 4
Preparation time 15 minutes
Cooking time 8–10 minutes

122
CALORIES
PER SERVING

Griddled aubergines with chilli toasts

- 2 teaspoons olive oil
- 2 aubergines, about 550 g (1 lb 2 oz) in total, cut into 5 mm (¼ inch) slices lengthways
- 50 g (2 oz) sun-dried tomatoes
- 2 garlic cloves, crushed
- 4 tablespoons lemon juice
- pepper
- 4 basil leaves, to garnish

Chilli toasts
- 4 slices of multigrain bread
- 1 tablespoon chilli-infused oil

1 To make the chilli toasts, remove the crusts from the bread, then cut each slice into 2 neat triangles. Brush each side of the bread with chilli-infused oil and place the bread on a baking sheet. Place in a preheated oven, 220°C (425°F), Gas Mark 7, for 8–10 minutes until crisp and golden.

2 Meanwhile, heat the oil in a ridged griddle pan. Season the aubergine slices with pepper and add to the pan with the sun-dried tomatoes and garlic and cook for about 4 minutes until beginning to soften. Turn the aubergines over and cook for a further 4 minutes, then add the lemon juice.

3 Remove the chilli toasts from the oven and serve with the aubergine and tomatoes piled high in the centre of 4 serving plates, seasoned with pepper and garnished with the basil leaves.

Serves 4
Preparation time 30 minutes
Cooking time 1½ hours

Stuffed red onions

- **4 large red onions, peeled**
- **2 tablespoons olive oil**
- **125 g (4 oz) button mushrooms, finely chopped**
- **75 g (3 oz) bulgar wheat**
- **1 tablespoon chopped parsley**
- **300 ml (½ pint) water**
- **1 tablespoon sultanas**
- **1 tablespoon grated Parmesan cheese (optional)**
- **salt and pepper**

1 Cut the top off each onion and scoop out the centre using a teaspoon, then finely chop the scooped-out onion. Heat the oil in a frying pan, add the chopped onion and fry until softened and golden brown. Add the mushrooms and cook, stirring, for a further 5 minutes.

2 Meanwhile, bring a large saucepan of water to the boil, add the onion cups and simmer for 10 minutes or until they begin to soften. Drain well.

3 Add the bulgar wheat, parsley, salt, pepper and measurement water to the mushrooms and boil for 5 minutes, then reduce the heat, cover and simmer for a further 30 minutes or until the grains have softened, adding extra water if necessary. Stir in the sultanas, then spoon the bulgar mixture into the onion cups.

4 Place the onions in a roasting tin and cover with foil. Bake in a preheated oven, 190°C (375°F), Gas Mark 5, for 30 minutes.

5 Remove from the oven and take off the foil. Sprinkle over the Parmesan, if using, and bake for a further 10 minutes. Serve hot.

Serves 6
Preparation time 5 minutes
Cooking time 30 minutes

170
CALORIES
PER SERVING

Quick red onion tagine

- **6 tablespoons olive oil**
- **750 g (1½ lb) red onions, finely sliced**
- **pinch of saffron threads**
- **¼ teaspoon ground ginger**
- **1 teaspoon ground black pepper**
- **½ teaspoon ground cinnamon**
- **1 tablespoon brown sugar**
- **150 ml (¼ pint) red wine**
- **chopped parsley or coriander, to garnish**

1 Heat the oil in a frying pan, add the onions, saffron, ginger, pepper, cinnamon and sugar and cook over a high heat for 2–3 minutes, stirring continuously. Add the red wine, continuing to stir, and boil rapidly until reduced to a syrupy consistency.

2 Transfer the onion mixture to a heavy-based casserole and cover with foil. Place in a preheated oven, 200°C (400°F), Gas Mark 6, for 20 minutes.

3 Remove from the oven and take off the foil, then bake for a further 5 minutes or until the onions are lightly glazed. Sprinkle with a little chopped parsley or coriander and serve hot or cold.

Serves 6
Preparation time 15 minutes
Cooking time 35–40 minutes

Spicy vegetable roast

- 1 teaspoon fennel seeds
- 1 teaspoon cumin seeds
- 1 teaspoon coriander seeds
- ½ teaspoon ground turmeric
- ½ teaspoon paprika
- 2 garlic cloves, chopped
- 3 tablespoons olive oil
- 500 g (1 lb) butternut squash, peeled, halved, deseeded and thickly sliced
- 4 small parsnips, about 425 g (14 oz) in total, cut into quarters
- 3 carrots, about 300 g (10 oz) in total, cut into thick strips
- salt and pepper

1 Crush the seeds using a pestle and mortar or the end of a rolling pin. Transfer to a large plastic bag and add the turmeric, paprika, garlic, oil and salt and pepper. Squeeze the bag to mix the contents together.

2 Add the vegetables to the plastic bag, grip the top edge to seal and toss together until the vegetables are coated with the spices.

3 Tip the vegetables into a roasting tin and bake in a preheated oven, 200°C (400°F), Gas Mark 6, for 35–40 minutes, turning once until browned and tender. Serve hot.

Serves 8
Preparation time 30 minutes, plus cooling and chilling
Cooking time 30–35 minutes

160
CALORIES
PER SERVING

Brûlée vanilla cheesecake

- butter, for greasing
- 3 x 200 g (7 oz) packets low-fat cream cheese
- 6 tablespoons granulated sweetener
- 1½ teaspoons vanilla extract
- finely grated rind of ½ orange
- 4 eggs, separated
- 1 tablespoon icing sugar, sifted
- 3 oranges, peeled and cut into segments, to serve

1 Lightly grease a 20 cm (8 inch) springform tin. Mix together the cream cheese, sweetener, vanilla extract, orange rind and egg yolks in a bowl until smooth.

2 Whisk the egg whites in a clean large bowl until soft peaks form, then fold a large spoonful into the cheese mixture to loosen it. Add the remaining egg whites and fold them in gently.

3 Pour the mixture into the prepared tin and level the surface. Bake in a preheated oven, 160°C (325°F), Gas Mark 3, for 30–35 minutes until well risen, golden brown and just set in the centre.

4 Turn off the oven and leave the cheesecake to cool for 15 minutes with the door slightly ajar. Remove from the oven, leave to cool, then chill for 4 hours. (The cheesecake will sink slightly as it cools.)

5 Run a knife around the cheesecake, loosen the tin and transfer to a serving plate. Dust the top with the icing sugar and caramelize the sugar with a cook's blowtorch. Serve within 30 minutes, while the sugar topping is still hard and brittle. Cut into 8 wedges and arrange on plates with the orange segments.

197
CALORIES
PER SERVING

Serves 4
Preparation time 10 minutes
Cooking time 20 minutes

Blueberry & lemon pancakes

- 125 g (4 oz) self-raising flour
- 1 teaspoon baking powder
- finely grated rind of ½ lemon
- 1 tablespoon caster sugar
- 1 egg, lightly beaten
- 1 tablespoon lemon juice
- 150 ml (¼ pint) semi-skimmed milk
- 125 g (4 oz) blueberries
- vegetable oil, for frying

1 Sift the flour and baking powder into a bowl and stir in the lemon rind and sugar. Add the egg and lemon juice and gradually whisk in the milk to make a smooth, thick batter. Stir in the blueberries.

2 Heat a griddle or large, nonstick frying pan and rub it with a piece of kitchen paper drizzled with a little oil. Drop spoonfuls of the mixture, spaced well apart, on the griddle or pan and cook for 2–3 minutes until bubbles form on the surface and the underside is golden-brown. Turn the pancakes over and cook on the other side. Wrap them in a tea towel and keep warm. Repeat with the remaining mixture to make 8 pancakes. Serve warm.

164 CALORIES PER SERVING

Fruit salad with banana cream

- **1 ruby grapefruit**
- **2 oranges**
- **2 kiwifruit, peeled**
- **1 ripe banana**
- **200 g (7 oz) low-fat fromage frais**
- **1 tablespoon clear honey**

1 Cut the top and bottom off the grapefruit with a serrated knife to reveal the flesh, then cut away the remaining peel and pith. Holding the fruit above a serving bowl, cut between the membranes to release the fruit segments. Repeat the process with the oranges.

2 Cut the kiwifruit in half, then into thin wedges. Mix with the citrus fruit. Cover and chill.

3 When ready to serve, mash the banana with a fork and stir it into the fromage frais with the honey. Spoon the fruit salad into 4 serving bowls and serve topped with the banana cream.

110
CALORIES
PER SERVING

Serves 6
Preparation time 20 minutes, plus soaking, cooling and chilling
Cooking time 8–9 minutes

Rhubarb & ginger parfait

- 400 g (13 oz) trimmed forced rhubarb
- 2.5 cm (1 inch) piece of fresh root ginger, peeled and finely chopped
- 5 tablespoons water
- 3 teaspoons powdered gelatine
- 4 egg yolks
- 6 tablespoons granulated sweetener
- 200 ml (7 fl oz) skimmed milk
- 2 egg whites
- 125 g (4 oz) low-fat crème fraîche
- a few drops pink food colouring (optional)
- orange rind, to decorate

1 Slice the rhubarb and put the pieces in a saucepan with the ginger and 2 tablespoons of the measurement water. Cover and simmer for 5 minutes until just tender and still bright pink. Mash or purée.

2 Put the remaining water in a small bowl and sprinkle over the gelatine, making sure that all the powder is absorbed by the water. Set aside to soak for 5 minutes.

3 Whisk the egg yolks and sweetener until just mixed. Pour the milk into a small saucepan and bring just to the boil. Gradually whisk the milk into the egg yolks, then pour the mixture back into the saucepan. Slowly bring the custard almost to the boil, stirring continuously, until it coats the back of the spoon. Do not allow the custard to boil or the eggs will curdle.

4 Take the pan off the heat and stir in the gelatine until it has dissolved. Pour into a bowl, stir in the cooked rhubarb and leave to cool.

5 Whisk the egg whites until stiff, moist peaks form. Fold the crème fraîche and a few drops of colouring, if used, into the cooled custard, then fold in the whisked whites. Spoon into 6 glasses and chill for 4 hours until lightly set. Decorate with orange rind just before serving.

Serves 4
Preparation time 5 minutes
Cooking time 25 minutes

127
CALORIES
PER SERVING

Fruity baked apples

- **4 large dessert apples**
- **125 g (4 oz) ready-to-eat dried fruit, such as cranberries, sultanas and apricots**
- **4 teaspoons demerara sugar**

1 Core the apples and score a line around the middle of each and arrange them in an ovenproof dish. Stuff the cored centre of the apples with the dried fruit.

2 Sprinkle over the sugar and bake in a preheated oven, 200°C (400°F), Gas Mark 6, for 25 minutes or until the apples are tender. Cut in half and serve.

Serves 12
Preparation time 15 minutes, plus proving
Cooking time 35 minutes

Olive & halloumi bread

- **500 g (1 lb) strong plain flour, plus extra for sifting**
- **7 g (¼ oz) sachet fast-action dried yeast**
- **pinch of salt**
- **2 tablespoons olive oil**
- **300 ml (½ pint) warm water**
- **1 onion, thinly sliced**
- **100 g (3½ oz) pitted olives**
- **75 g (3 oz) low-fat halloumi cheese, chopped**
- **2 tablespoons chopped parsley**

1 Place the flour, yeast and salt in a large bowl. Combine half the oil with the measured water in a jug and stir into the flour to form a dough.

2 Turn the dough out onto a lightly floured surface and knead for 5 minutes until smooth and elastic. Place in a lightly oiled bowl, cover with a damp cloth and set aside in a warm place for about 1 hour until doubled in size.

3 Meanwhile, heat the remaining oil in a frying pan, add the onion and fry for 7–8 minutes until softened and golden. Leave to cool.

4 Turn the risen dough out onto the floured surface and add the remaining ingredients, including the onion, kneading it into the dough. Shape into an oval, place on a lightly floured baking sheet and leave to rise for 1 hour.

5 When the loaf has risen, slash a few cuts in the top with a sharp knife, sift over a little flour, then bake in a preheated oven, 220°C (425°F), Gas Mark 7, for about 25 minutes until hollow-sounding when tapped. Transfer to a wire rack to cool.

Makes 16
Preparation time 10 minutes
Cooking time 35 minutes

156 CALORIES PER SERVING

Breakfast cereal bars

- 100 g (3½ oz) butter, softened, plus extra for greasing
- 25 g (1 oz) light muscovado sugar
- 2 tablespoons golden syrup
- 125 g (4 oz) millet flakes
- 50 g (2 oz) quinoa
- 50 g (2 oz) dried cherries or cranberries
- 75 g (3 oz) sultanas
- 25 g (1 oz) sunflower seeds
- 25 g (1 oz) sesame seeds
- 25 g (1 oz) linseeds
- 40 g (1½ oz) unsweetened desiccated coconut
- 2 eggs, lightly beaten

1 Beat together the butter, sugar and syrup in a large bowl until creamy. Add all the remaining ingredients and beat well until combined.

2 Turn the mixture into a greased 28 × 20 cm (11 × 8 inch) shallow rectangular baking tin and level the surface with the back of a dessertspoon.

3 Bake in a preheated oven, 180°C (350°F), Gas Mark 4, for 35 minutes until deep golden. Leave to cool in the tin. Turn out on to a wooden board and carefully cut into 16 fingers using a serrated knife. The bars can be stored in an airtight container for up to 5 days.

200
CALORIES
PER SERVING

Makes 12
Preparation time 15 minutes
Cooking time 20–30 minutes

Apple & blackberry muffins

- 6 tablespoons light muscovado sugar
- 1 red apple, about 150 g (5 oz), cored and diced
- 200 g (7 oz) blackberries, roughly chopped
- 1 teaspoon ground cinnamon
- 250 g (8 oz) plain wholemeal flour
- 4 teaspoons baking powder
- 2 eggs, beaten
- 125 ml (4 fl oz) semi-skimmed milk
- 125 ml (4 fl oz) rapeseed oil, plus extra for cooking

1 Mix together the sugar, apple, blackberries and cinnamon in a bowl.

2 Sift the flour and baking powder into a separate bowl and make a well in the centre. Mix together the eggs, milk and oil in a jug, then pour into the well and stir until blended. Stir in the fruit mixture, taking care not to over-mix. Divide the mixture among the sections of a lightly oiled or paper case-lined 12-hole muffin tin.

3 Bake in a preheated oven, 200°C (400°F), Gas Mark 6, for 20–30 minutes or until a skewer inserted into the centre comes out clean. Transfer the muffins to a wire rack to cool. The muffins can be stored in an airtight container for up to 3 days.

Makes 12 slices
Preparation time 15 minutes, plus cooling
Cooking time 15–20 minutes

122 CALORIES PER SERVING

Baked almond & apricot cake

- **4 eggs**
- **125 g (4 oz) caster sugar**
- **½ teaspoon almond extract**
- **50 g (2 oz) plain flour**
- **75 g (3 oz) ground almonds**
- **butter, for greasing**

Apricot filling
- **125 g (4 oz) ready-to-eat dried apricots**
- **150–200 ml (5–7 fl oz) water**
- **125 g (4 oz) low-fat fromage frais**

1 Put the eggs, sugar and almond extract in a large bowl and whisk until thick and frothy. Sift the flour into the bowl and gently fold in with the ground almonds.

2 Divide the cake mixture between 2 lined and lightly greased 18 cm (7 inch) round cake tins. Bake in a preheated oven, 180°C (350°F), Gas Mark 4, for 15-20 minutes. Leave to cool in the tins for 10 minutes, then loosen the edges with a knife and turn out on to a wire rack to cool.

3 Meanwhile, make the filling, put the apricots in a small saucepan with the measurement water, cover and simmer for 10 minutes until softened. Transfer to a blender or food processor and blend until smooth. Leave to cool, then sandwich the cake together with the apricot filling and the fromage frais.

120 CALORIES PER SERVING

Makes 8
Preparation time 10 minutes
Cooking time 18 minutes

Rhubarb bakes

- **50 g (2 oz) margarine**
- **2 tablespoons golden syrup**
- **1 tablespoon light muscovado sugar**
- **75 g (3 oz) rolled oats**
- **50 g (2 oz) wholemeal self-raising flour, sifted**
- **pinch of ground ginger**
- **25 g (1 oz) pecan nuts, chopped**
- **6 tablespoons rhubarb compote or stewed rhubarb**

1 Put the margarine, syrup and sugar in a saucepan and heat gently until the sugar is dissolved. Stir in the oats, flour, ginger and nuts and combine well.

2 Spoon two-thirds of the mixture into a 15 cm (6 inch) square, nonstick baking tin and gently press down. Spoon over the rhubarb, sprinkle over the remaining oat mixture and press down lightly.

3 Bake in a preheated oven, 180°C (350°F), Gas Mark 4, for 15 minutes until golden. Leave to cool in the tin, marking the mixture into 8 rectangles while still warm.

300
CALORIES
AND UNDER

Serves 4
Preparation time 20 minutes
Cooking time 40–50 minutes

Spicy lentil & tomato soup

- 1 tablespoon vegetable oil
- 1 large onion, finely chopped
- 2 garlic cloves, finely chopped
- 1 small green chilli, deseeded and finely chopped
- 250 g (8 oz) red lentils, washed and drained
- 1 bay leaf
- 3 celery sticks, thinly sliced
- 3 carrots, thinly sliced
- 1 leek, trimmed and thinly sliced
- 1.5 litres (2½ pints) vegetable stock
- 400 g (13 oz) can chopped tomatoes
- 2 tablespoons tomato purée
- ½ tablespoon ground turmeric
- ½ teaspoon ground ginger
- 1 tablespoon coriander leaves
- pepper

1 Heat the oil in a large saucepan, add the onion, garlic and chilli and fry gently for 4–5 minutes until softened.

2 Add the lentils, bay leaf, celery, carrots, leek and vegetable stock. Cover and bring to the boil, then reduce the heat and simmer for 30–40 minutes. Remove the bay leaf.

3 Stir in the tomatoes, tomato purée, turmeric, ginger, coriander and pepper to taste. Leave to cool slightly, then transfer to a blender or food processor and blend until smooth, adding more stock or water if necessary. Return to the pan and reheat gently before serving.

Serves 4
Preparation time 10 minutes
Cooking time 25–30 minutes

300
CALORIES
PER SERVING

Hearty seafood soup

- 15 g (½ oz) butter
- 1 onion, chopped
- 1 bay leaf
- 2 celery sticks, finely sliced
- 300 g (10 oz) floury potatoes, peeled and cubed
- 450 ml (¾ pint) skimmed milk
- 450 ml (¾ pint) fish stock
- 375 g (12 oz) mixed boneless, skinless fish fillets, such as smoked haddock, cod and salmon, cubed
- 100 g (3½ oz) cooked peeled prawns
- 100 g (3½ oz) frozen peas
- 100 g (3½ oz) frozen sweetcorn
- salt and pepper

To garnish
- 3 tablespoons chopped parsley
- 2 tomatoes, finely chopped

1 Melt the butter in a large saucepan, add the onion, bay leaf, celery and potatoes and fry for 3–4 minutes.

2 Add the milk and fish stock and bring to the boil, then reduce the heat, cover and simmer for 15–20 minutes until the potatoes are cooked.

3 Add the fish, prawns, peas and sweetcorn and simmer for a further 5 minutes or until the fish is cooked through.

4 Season with salt and pepper and serve scattered with the parsley and chopped tomatoes.

285
CALORIES
PER SERVING

Serves 6
Preparation time 10 minutes
Cooking time 8 minutes

Green bean & asparagus salad

- 250 g (8 oz) fine green beans, trimmed
- 400 g (13 oz) asparagus, trimmed
- 6 eggs
- 100 g (3½ oz) rocket
- 75 g (3 oz) pitted black olives
- 75 g (3 oz) Parmesan cheese shavings

Dressing
- 5 tablespoons olive oil
- 3 teaspoons black olive pesto or tapenade
- 3 teaspoons balsamic vinegar
- salt and pepper

1 Put the green beans in a steamer set over a saucepan of boiling water, cover and cook for 3 minutes. Add the asparagus and cook for a further 5 minutes until the vegetables are just tender.

2 Meanwhile, put the eggs in a small saucepan, cover with cold water and bring to the boil. Simmer for 6 minutes until still soft in the centre.

3 Make the dressing by combining the oil, pesto or tapenade and vinegar in a small bowl with a little salt and pepper.

4 Arrange the rocket in the centre of 6 serving plates. Drain and rinse the eggs with cold water. Drain again, gently peel away the shells and halve each egg. Place 2 halves on each mound of rocket. Arrange the beans and asparagus around the edge, then drizzle with the dressing. Add the olives and top with the Parmesan shavings. Serve immediately.

Serves 4
Preparation time 15 minutes
Cooking time 2½ minutes

300
CALORIES
PER SERVING

Warm scallop salad with strawberry dressing

- **12 king scallops, without corals, each cut into 3 slices**
- **juice of 1 lemon**
- **250 g (8 oz) mixed salad leaves**
- **20 wild strawberries or 8 larger strawberries, sliced, to garnish**
- **salt and pepper**

Dressing
- **250 g (8 oz) wild strawberries, hulled**
- **2 tablespoons balsamic vinegar**
- **1 tablespoon lemon juice**
- **50 ml (2 fl oz) olive oil**

Leek garnish
- **1 tablespoon olive oil**
- **3 leeks, trimmed and cut into matchstick strips**

1 Place the dressing ingredients in a blender or food processor and blend until smooth. Pass the purée through a fine sieve or muslin cloth to remove the pips and set aside.

2 Season the scallops with salt, pepper and the lemon juice.

3 To make the garnish, heat the oil in a nonstick frying pan over a high heat, add the leeks and fry for 1 minute or until golden brown. Remove from the pan and set aside. In the same pan, fry the scallop slices for 20–30 seconds on each side.

4 Divide the salad leaves evenly among 4 serving plates. Arrange the scallop slices over the salad.

5 In a small pan, gently heat the strawberry dressing for 20–30 seconds, then pour over the scallops and salad leaves. Scatter over the leek garnish and sliced strawberries. Sprinkle with a little pepper and serve.

Serves 4
Preparation time 30 minutes
Cooking time 13 minutes

Thai mussel curry with ginger

- ½–1 large red chilli, to taste
- 2 shallots, quartered
- 1 lemon grass stem
- 2.5 cm (1 inch) piece of fresh root ginger, peeled and chopped
- 1 tablespoon sunflower oil
- 400 ml (14 fl oz) can reduced-fat coconut milk
- 4–5 kaffir lime leaves
- 150 ml (¼ pint) fish stock
- 2 teaspoons Thai fish sauce
- 1.5 kg (3 lb) fresh mussels, soaked in cold water
- small bunch of coriander, torn into pieces, to garnish

1 Halve the chilli and keep the seeds for extra heat, if liked. Put the chilli, shallots and lemon grass into a food processor with the ginger and process together until finely chopped.

2 Heat the oil in large, deep saucepan, add the finely chopped ingredients and fry over a medium heat for 5 minutes, stirring until softened. Add the coconut milk, kaffir lime leaves, fish stock and fish sauce and cook for 3 minutes. Set aside until ready to finish.

3 Meanwhile, pick over the mussels and discard any that are opened or have cracked shells. Scrub with a small nailbrush, remove any barnacles and pull off the small, hairy beards. Put them in a bowl of clean water and leave until ready to cook.

4 Reheat the coconut milk mixture. Drain the mussels and add to the mixture. Cover the pan with a lid and cook for about 5 minutes until the mussel shells have opened.

5 Spoon the mussels and the coconut sauce into bowls, discarding any mussels that have not opened. Garnish with the coriander.

Serves 4
Preparation time 10 minutes
Cooking time 20 minutes

293
CALORIES
PER SERVING

Scallops with white bean purée

- 2 x 400 g (13 oz) cans cannellini beans, drained and rinsed
- 2 garlic cloves
- 200 ml (7 fl oz) vegetable stock
- 2 tablespoons chopped parsley
- 2 teaspoons olive oil
- 16 baby leeks
- 3 tablespoons water
- 16 large scallops
- parsley sprigs, to garnish

1 Place the beans, garlic and stock in a saucepan and bring to the boil, then reduce the heat and simmer for 10 minutes. Remove from the heat, drain off any excess liquid, then mash with a potato masher and stir in the parsley. Keep warm.

2 Heat half the oil in a nonstick frying pan, add the leeks and fry for 2 minutes, then add the measured water. Cover and simmer for 5–6 minutes until tender.

3 Meanwhile, heat the remaining oil in a small frying pan, add the scallops and fry for 1 minute on each side until just cooked through. Serve with the white bean purée and leeks and garnish with parsley sprigs.

221
CALORIES
PER SERVING

Serves 4
Preparation time 15 minutes
Cooking time 20 minutes

Cod with chilli butter beans & tomatoes

- 2 teaspoons vegetable oil
- 1 celery stick, finely diced
- 1 onion, finely chopped
- 1 garlic clove, crushed, or 1 teaspoon minced garlic
- 400 g (13 oz) can tomatoes, undrained and mashed
- 2 tablespoons tomato purée
- 300 g (10 oz) can butter beans, rinsed and drained
- 1 green chilli, deseeded and finely chopped
- 125 ml (4 fl oz) dry white wine
- 500 g (1 lb) cod fillet or any boneless white fish fillets, cut into cubes
- pepper
- 2 tablespoons chopped parsley, to garnish

1 Heat the oil in a nonstick saucepan, add the celery, onion and garlic and cook for about 5 minutes until softened. Add the tomatoes, tomato purée, beans and chilli and simmer, uncovered, for 10 minutes.

2 Meanwhile, heat the wine in a separate saucepan. Add the fish and poach gently for about 3–4 minutes until just cooked through.

3 Combine the fish and its cooking liquid with the bean and tomato mixture and heat through. Season with pepper and serve garnished with parsley.

Serves 4
Preparation time 30 minutes
Cooking time 8 minutes

234
CALORIES
PER SERVING

Plaice parcels with orange & radicchio salad

- 1 fennel bulb, about 360 g (11½ oz), trimmed and finely chopped
- 2 red chillies, deseeded and chopped
- 4 tablespoons lemon juice
- 2 teaspoons olive oil
- 4 plaice fillets, about 650 g (1 lb 6 oz) in total
- small handful of dill, chopped
- ½ lemon, cut into wedges, to serve

Orange and radicchio salad
- 2 large oranges
- 200 g (7 oz) red radicchio leaves

1 Mix together the fennel, chillies, lemon juice and oil in a non-metallic bowl and set aside.

2 Cut 4 sheets of nonstick baking paper, each 35 × 18 cm (14 × 7 inches), and fold them in half widthways. Lay ½ sheet over a plate and arrange a fish fillet on one side of the fold. Sprinkle over some chopped dill and fold over the paper to enclose the filling. Fold in the edges and pleat to secure. Repeat with the remaining fish.

3 Place the wrapped fish on a baking sheet and bake in a preheated oven, 220°C (425°F), Gas Mark 7, for about 8 minutes or until the paper is puffed up and brown.

4 Meanwhile, make the salad. Cut the top and bottom off the oranges with a serrated knife to reveal the flesh, then cut away the remaining peel and pith. Holding the fruit above a serving bowl, cut between the membranes to release the fruit segments. Add the radicchio and gently toss together.

5 Place each fish parcel on a large plate and cut an X-shaped slit in the top and curl back the paper, or pull the paper apart to open the parcel, releasing a fragrant puff of steam. Serve with bowls of the fennel and chilli mixture and the radicchio and orange salad, and lemon wedges.

252
CALORIES
PER SERVING

Serves 6
Preparation time 15 minutes
Cooking time 12–13 minutes

Grilled sea bass with cherry tomatoes

- 1 tablespoon olive oil
- 1 onion, finely chopped
- 300 g (10 oz) cherry tomatoes, halved
- 2 large pinches of saffron threads (optional)
- 150 ml (¼ pint) dry white wine
- 125 ml (4 fl oz) fish stock
- grated rind of 1 lemon, the rest halved and thinly sliced
- 12 small sea bass fillets, about 100 g (3½ oz) each, rinsed in cold water
- 1 teaspoon fennel seeds
- salt and pepper
- basil or oregano leaves, to garnish (optional)

1 Heat the oil in a frying pan, add the onion and fry for 5 minutes until softened and lightly browned. Add the tomatoes, saffron, if using, wine and stock and stir in the lemon rind and a little salt and pepper. Bring to the boil and cook for 2 minutes.

2 Pour the mixture into the base of a foil-lined grill pan, add the lemon slices and set aside until ready to cook.

3 Arrange the fish fillets, skin side up, on top of the tomato mixture. Use a teaspoon to scoop some of the juices over the skin, then sprinkle with salt and pepper and the fennel seeds.

4 Cook under a preheated grill for 5–6 minutes until the skin is crispy and the fish flakes easily when pressed with a knife. Serve sprinkled with basil or oregano leaves, if liked.

Serves 4
Preparation time 15 minutes
Cooking time 15 minutes

300
CALORIES
PER SERVING

Honey-glazed tuna

- 4 tuna steaks, about 125 g (4 oz) each
- 2 teaspoons olive oil

Glaze
- 1 tablespoon honey
- 2 tablespoons wholegrain mustard
- 1 teaspoon tomato purée
- 2 tablespoons orange juice
- 1 tablespoon red wine vinegar or balsamic vinegar
- pepper

Parsnip purée
- 1 parsnip, cut into chunks
- 2 potatoes, cut into chunks
- 50 g (2 oz) natural yogurt
- 2 teaspoons horseradish sauce (optional)

1 Put all the ingredients for the glaze in a small saucepan and bring to the boil, then reduce the heat and simmer until the mixture reduces and is of a glaze consistency. Keep hot.

2 Make the parsnip purée. Steam the parsnip and potatoes until tender. Drain, if necessary, and place in a food processor or blender with the yogurt, horseradish sauce, if using, and pepper to taste. Process until blended. Keep warm or reheat prior to serving.

3 Brush the tuna with the oil. Cook on a preheated, very hot griddle or barbecue, or in a frying pan or under a grill, for 1–2 minutes. Turn the tuna over and spoon over the glaze. Cook for a further 1–2 minutes until still moist and slightly pink in the centre.

4 Spoon a mound of the parsnip purée on to 4 serving plates and top each with a tuna steak. Serve with any remaining glaze spooned over.

Serves 4
Preparation time 5 minutes
Cooking time 25 minutes

Steamed fish with ginger & coconut milk

- **750 g (1½ lb) fish fillets such as salmon, cod or mullet, skinned**
- **½ teaspoon salt**
- **2 tablespoons vegetable oil**
- **3 garlic cloves, finely sliced**
- **3½ oz (90 g) onions, finely sliced**
- **1½ tablespoons oyster sauce**
- **6 tablespoons coconut milk**
- **2.5 cm (1 inch) cube fresh root ginger, peeled and finely sliced into slivers**
- **2 spring onions, finely sliced**
- **4 medium mushrooms, finely sliced**
- **4–5 tablespoons roasted peanuts**
- **pepper**

1 Wash the fish and pat it dry. Put the fish onto a heatproof dish or plate that will fit into your steamer or on a rack in a pan. Rub the fish with the salt and season with pepper.

2 Place a sieve over a bowl and cover a plate in kitchen paper. Heat the oil in a frying pan over a medium-low heat. When the oil is hot, put in the garlic slivers and fry until golden. Remove with a slotted spoon and place in the sieve, then transfer onto the kitchen paper. Repeat with the onion slices.

3 Combine the oyster sauce with 2 tablespoons of the coconut milk and spread the mixture evenly over the fish. Scatter the ginger, spring onions, mushrooms, fried garlic and half the fried onions over the top.

4 Place the plate with the fish on the rack in the steamer and cover. Build up steam over a high heat for 2 minutes, then turn down the heat to medium-high and steam the fish for a further 18 minutes.

5 Carefully lift the plate from the steamer. Transfer some of the sauce around the fish to a small pan, add the rest of the coconut milk and heat gently.

6 Pour over the fish and scatter with the remaining onions and the peanuts. Serve immediately.

Serves 4
Preparation time 30 minutes
Cooking time 25 minutes

240
CALORIES
PER SERVING

Seafood zarzuela

- **500 g (1 lb) tomatoes**
- **1 tablespoon olive oil**
- **1 large onion, finely chopped**
- **2 garlic cloves, finely chopped**
- **½ teaspoon smoked paprika**
- **1 red pepper, cored, deseeded and diced**
- **200 ml (7 fl oz) fish stock**
- **150 ml (¼ pint) dry white wine**
- **2 large pinches of saffron threads**
- **4 small bay leaves**
- **500 g (1 lb) fresh mussels, soaked in cold water**
- **200 g (7 oz) raw squid, cleaned and rinsed in cold water**
- **375 g (12 oz) skinless cod loin, cubed**
- **salt and pepper**

1 Put the tomatoes in a large saucepan and pour over enough boiling water to cover, then leave for about 1 minute. Drain and cool in a bowl of ice-cold water, then drain again. Skin the tomatoes and roughly chop the flesh.

2 Heat the oil in a large saucepan, add the onion and fry for 5 minutes until softened. Stir in the garlic and paprika and cook, stirring, for a further 1 minute. Stir in the tomatoes, red pepper, stock, wine and saffron. Add the bay leaves, season with salt and pepper and bring to the boil. Cover and simmer gently for 10 minutes, then remove the pan from the heat and set aside.

3 Meanwhile, discard any mussels that are opened or have cracked shells. Scrub with a small nailbrush, remove any barnacles and pull off any small, hairy beards. Put them in a bowl of clean water and leave until ready to cook. Separate the squid tubes from the tentacles, then slice the tubes.

4 Reheat the tomato sauce if necessary, add the cod and the sliced squid and cook for 2 minutes. Drain the mussels and add to the pan, cover and cook for 4 minutes. Add the squid tentacles and cook for a further 2 minutes until the fish is cooked through and all the mussel shells have opened. Gently stir, then serve, discarding any mussels that have not opened.

Serves 2
Preparation time 15 minutes, plus cooling
Cooking time 8–10 minutes

Asian steamed chicken salad

- 2 skinless chicken breast fillets, about 150 g (5 oz) each
- ¼ small Chinese cabbage, finely shredded
- ½ large carrot, grated
- 125 g (4 oz) bean sprouts
- handful of coriander, finely chopped
- handful of mint, finely chopped
- ½ red chilli, deseeded and finely sliced (optional)

Dressing
- 40 ml (1½ fl oz) sunflower oil
- juice of 1 lime
- ¾ tablespoon Thai fish sauce
- 1½ tablespoons light soy sauce
- ½ tablespoon peeled and finely chopped fresh root ginger

1 Put the chicken in the top of a steamer, cover and cook for about 8 minutes or until the chicken is cooked through. Alternatively, poach the chicken in a pan of simmering water for 8–10 minutes until cooked through and tender. Remove from the pan and leave until cool enough to handle.

2 Meanwhile, make the dressing by placing all the ingredients in a screw-top jar, adding the lid and shaking until well combined.

3 Cut or tear the cooked chicken into strips and mix with 1 tablespoon of the dressing in a bowl. Leave to cool completely.

4 Toss together all the vegetables, herbs and chilli, if using, in a large bowl, then divide between 2 serving plates. Scatter over the cold chicken and serve immediately with the remaining dressing.

Serves 4
Preparation time 10 minutes, plus marinating
Cooking time 30 minutes

Chicken fillets with soy glaze

- 4 chicken breast fillets, about 125 g (4 oz) each
- 4 tablespoons dark soy sauce
- 2 tablespoons light muscovado sugar
- 2 garlic cloves, crushed
- 2 tablespoons white wine vinegar
- 100 ml (3½ fl oz) freshly squeezed orange juice
- pepper

1 Lay the chicken fillets on a chopping board and slice each in half horizontally. Place in a large, shallow ovenproof dish, in which the fillets fit snugly.

2 Mix together the soy sauce, sugar, garlic, vinegar, orange juice and pepper and pour the mixture over the chicken. Cover and leave to marinate in the refrigerator until ready to cook.

3 Bake in a preheated oven, 180°C (350°F), Gas Mark 4, for 30 minutes until the chicken is cooked through. Serve the chicken with the cooking juices spooned over.

275
CALORIES
PER SERVING

Serves 4
Preparation time 10 minutes
Cooking time 35–45 minutes

Baked herby chicken & vegetables

- 500 g (1 lb) new potatoes
- 4 chicken breast fillets, about 125 g (4 oz) each
- 6 tablespoons fresh mixed herbs, such as parsley, chives, chervil and mint
- 1 garlic clove, crushed
- 6 tablespoons crème fraîche
- 8 baby leeks
- 2 heads of chicory, halved lengthways
- 150 ml (¼ pint) chicken stock
- pepper

1 Cook the potatoes in a saucepan of boiling water for 12–15 minutes until tender. Drain, then cut into bite-sized pieces.

2 Make a slit lengthways down the side of each chicken breast to form a pocket, ensuring that you do not cut all the way through. Mix together the herbs, garlic and crème fraîche, season well with pepper, then spoon a little into each chicken pocket.

3 Place the leeks, chicory and potatoes in an ovenproof dish. Pour over the stock, then lay the chicken breasts on top. Spoon over the remaining crème fraîche mixture.

4 Bake in a preheated oven, 200°C (400°F), Gas Mark 6, for 25–30 minutes until the chicken is cooked through and the vegetables are tender. Serve hot.

Serves 4
Preparation time 10 minutes
Cooking time 11–12 minutes

227 CALORIES PER SERVING

Easy corned beef hash

- 1 teaspoon vegetable oil
- 1 onion, roughly chopped
- 350 g (11½ oz) cooked new potatoes, roughly chopped
- 300 g (10 oz) corned beef, roughly chopped
- 1 tablespoon chopped parsley
- Worcestershire sauce, to taste
- pepper

1 Heat the oil in a large, nonstick frying pan, add the onion and fry for 5 minutes until softened. Add the potatoes and corned beef and cook for a further 6–7 minutes, turning the mixture occasionally so that parts of it become crisp.

2 Add the parsley and stir through the mixture, season to taste with Worcestershire sauce and pepper and serve immediately.

Top tip

It takes 20 minutes for your brain to register that your stomach is full, so eating slowly is a great trick to stop you from overeating on your 'off' days.

Serves 4
Preparation time 15 minutes
Cooking time 11–12 minutes

Tamarind & lemon grass beef

- 1 tablespoon olive oil
- 500 g (1 lb) lean beef, cut into strips
- 2 lemon grass stalks, chopped
- 6 shallots, chopped
- 2 green chillies, chopped
- 3 tablespoons tamarind paste
- 2 tablespoons lime juice
- 2 teaspoons fish sauce
- 2 teaspoons brown sugar
- 200 g (7 oz) shredded green papaya

1 Heat the oil in a wok or frying pan over a high heat, add the beef and stir-fry for 2–3 minutes.

2 Add the lemon grass, shallots and chillies and stir-fry for a further 5 minutes or until the meat is well browned.

3 Add the tamarind paste, lime juice, fish sauce, sugar and green papaya and stir-fry for a further 4 minutes. Serve immediately.

Top tip

If hunger is getting the better of you, try taking a brisk walk round the block or running up and down the stairs five times – anything to take your mind of that grumbling tummy.

Serves 4
Preparation time 10 minutes
Cooking time 7–8 minutes

290 CALORIES PER SERVING

Seared steak with Parmesan & rocket

- 3 tablespoons light olive oil
- 2 red onions, thickly sliced
- 500 g (1 lb) sirloin steak, cut into 8 steaks
- 150 g (5 oz) rocket
- 125 g (4 oz) Parmesan cheese shavings
- 3 tablespoons flat-leaf parsley
- 2 tablespoons balsamic vinegar
- pepper

1 Heat 1 tablespoon of the oil in a frying pan over a medium heat, add the onions and cook for 5 minutes or until golden. Remove the onions from the pan and keep warm.

2 Increase the heat to high and add the steaks to the frying pan. Cook for about ½–1 minute on each side or until sealed and seared.

3 Toss together the rocket, Parmesan shavings, parsley, balsamic vinegar, black pepper and the remaining oil in a bowl.

4 Place a steak on each of 4 serving plates, add some of the salad mixture and then another steak. Serve topped with the fried onions.

Serves 4
Preparation time 25 minutes, plus chilling
Cooking time 35–40 minutes

Kofta curry

- 1 small onion, chopped
- 2 teaspoons peeled and grated fresh root ginger
- 3 garlic cloves, roughly chopped
- 3 tablespoons coriander leaves
- 325 g (11 oz) lean minced lamb or beef
- ½ teaspoon chilli powder
- ¼ teaspoon garam masala
- 1 tablespoon cornflour

Sauce
- 1 tablespoon vegetable oil
- 1 small onion, finely chopped
- ¼ teaspoon cumin seeds
- 2–3 green cardamom pods
- 1 teaspoon ginger paste
- 1 teaspoon garlic paste
- ½ teaspoon chilli powder
- ¼ teaspoon ground turmeric
- ¼ teaspoon garam masala
- 75 g (3 oz) tomatoes, chopped
- 1 tablespoon natural yogurt
- 450 ml (¾ pint) water
- 1 green chilli, deseeded and finely chopped
- 2 tablespoons coriander leaves

1 To make the koftas, place the onion, ginger, garlic and coriander in a food processor or blender and process until blended. Put the mince in a bowl and add the blended mixture, spices and cornflour, then knead until mixed. Cover and chill for 10–15 minutes to allow the spices to infuse.

2 To make the sauce, heat the oil in a heavy-based saucepan, add the onion and fry gently for 5 minutes. Add the cumin and cardamom and cook for about 2 minutes until the onions are browned, then add the garlic and ginger paste and remaining spices. Cook for about 5 minutes until the spices darken, adding a little water when necessary. Add the tomatoes and yogurt, stirring continuously.

3 Meanwhile, divide the kofta mixture into 16 equal portions and roll each portion into a smooth round ball. Cook the koftas under a preheated medium grill for 10 minutes, turning once to drain off all the excess fat.

4 Add the koftas to the sauce mixture. Cook, stirring, for about 2 minutes, then add the measurement water, cover and simmer for 20–25 minutes. Stir in the chilli and coriander, adding a little boiling water if necessary. Serve hot.

Serves 4
Preparation time 10 minutes, plus marinating
Cooking time 10–12 minutes

261
CALORIES
PER SERVING

Pan-fried spiced lamb & flageolet beans

- ½ teaspoon ground cumin
- ½ teaspoon ground coriander
- pinch of chilli powder
- 1 tablespoon olive oil
- 4 lean lamb steaks
- 1 onion, sliced
- 1 garlic clove, crushed
- 4 tablespoons lemon juice
- 400 g (13 oz) can flageolet beans, rinsed and drained
- 1 tablespoon chopped mint
- 2 tablespoons low-fat crème fraîche

1 Mix together the cumin, coriander, chilli powder and half the oil in a non-metallic bowl. Add the lamb, coat it in the spices and leave to marinate for 10 minutes.

2 Heat the remaining oil in a nonstick pan, add the onion and garlic and fry for 3–4 minutes until softened.

3 Add the lamb and the marinade and fry the steaks for 2–3 minutes on each side or until cooked to your liking.

4 Add the lemon juice, flageolet beans, mint and crème fraîche and simmer for 1 minute until warmed through. Serve immediately.

Serves 4
Preparation time 10 minutes, plus marinating
Cooking time 2–2½ hours

Lamb shanks with spiced beans & balsamic onions

- 4 lamb shanks, about 1.25 kg (2½ lb) in total, fat removed
- 4–5 rosemary sprigs
- 2 garlic cloves, thinly sliced
- 4 small red onions, halved
- 3 tablespoons balsamic vinegar

Marinade
- small bunch of thyme, leaves removed from stalks
- 3 whole cardamom pods
- 1 bay leaf
- pinch of saffron threads
- 4 tablespoons lemon juice
- salt and pepper

Spiced beans
- 2 teaspoons rapeseed oil
- ½ teaspoon black mustard seeds
- ½ teaspoon onion seeds
- 1 tablespoon tomato purée
- pinch of ground turmeric
- ¼–½ teaspoon chilli powder
- 2 × 300 g (10 oz) cans pinto beans, rinsed and drained
- 2 tablespoons chopped coriander leaves, plus extra to garnish

1 Place the shanks in a ceramic roasting tin, make slits in each shank and push in sprigs of rosemary and slices of garlic.

2 Mix together the marinade ingredients in a non-metallic bowl. Coat the lamb shanks, cover with foil and leave to marinate in the refrigerator for at least 1 hour.

3 Cook the lamb in a preheated oven, 160°C (325°F), Gas Mark 3, for 2–2½ hours, basting every 45 minutes or so, until the meat is tender.

4 Meanwhile, place the halved onions, cut sides up, in a heatproof dish, pour over the vinegar and cook under a preheated medium grill for about 20 minutes until soft.

5 Prepare the beans. Heat the oil in a frying pan, add the mustard and onion seeds and cook over a low heat, letting them pop for a few seconds. Stir in the tomato purée, turmeric and chilli powder. Add the beans and a few tablespoons of hot water. Cover and cook for a few minutes. Stir in the coriander and remove from the heat.

6 Serve the lamb with the spiced beans and grilled red onions, sprinkled with chopped coriander.

Serves 4
Preparation time 10 minutes
Cooking time 12–14 minutes

280
CALORIES
PER SERVING

Lamb cutlets with herbed crust

- **12 lean lamb cutlets, about 40 g (1½ oz) each**
- **2 tablespoons pesto**
- **3 tablespoons granary breadcrumbs**
- **1 tablespoon chopped walnuts, toasted**
- **1 teaspoon vegetable oil**
- **2 garlic cloves, crushed**
- **625 g (1¼ lb) greens, finely shredded and blanched**

1 Heat a nonstick frying pan or griddle until hot, add the cutlets and cook for 1 minute on each side, then transfer to a baking sheet.

2 Mix together the pesto, breadcrumbs and walnuts in a bowl. Spoon the mixture on to one side of the cutlets, pressing down lightly. Place in a preheated oven, 200°C (400°F), Gas Mark 6, for 10–12 minutes.

3 Meanwhile, heat the oil in a frying pan or wok, add the garlic and stir-fry for 1 minute, then add the greens and stir-fry for a further 3–4 minutes until tender. Serve the lamb with the greens.

265
CALORIES
PER SERVING

Serves 4
Preparation time 10 minutes, plus marinating
Cooking time 20 minutes

Marinated pork fillet

- **2 fillets of pork, about 250 g (8 oz) each**
- **1 tablespoon linseeds**
- **150 ml (¼ pint) dry white wine**

Marinade
- **1 cinnamon stick**
- **2 tablespoons soy sauce**
- **2 garlic cloves, crushed**
- **1 teaspoon peeled and grated fresh root ginger**
- **1 tablespoon clear honey**
- **1 teaspoon crushed coriander seeds**
- **1 teaspoon sesame oil**

1 Mix together the marinade ingredients, then place the pork fillets in a shallow non-metallic dish and cover evenly with the marinade. Cover and leave to marinate in the refrigerator for at least 2–3 hours or preferably overnight.

2 When ready to cook, drain the pork, reserving the marinade. Lay the meat in the linseeds on both sides so it is evenly covered. Place on a baking sheet or in a roasting tin and seal it over a high heat on the hob, then roast in a preheated oven, 180°C (350°F), Gas Mark 4, for 18–20 minutes or until golden brown.

3 Meanwhile, remove the cinnamon stick from the marinade and pour the liquid into a nonstick pan. Add the white wine and bring to the boil. Reduce the heat and simmer until it has the consistency of a sticky glaze. Remove from the heat and set aside.

4 Remove the pork from the oven and cut into 5 mm (¼ inch) slices. Serve drizzled with the glaze.

Serves 4
Preparation time 15 minutes
Cooking time 16 minutes

271
CALORIES
PER SERVING

Wild venison steaks with ratatouille

- 4 venison steaks, about 125 g (4 oz) each
- 2 tablespoons olive oil
- 1 garlic clove, crushed
- 1 red onion, chopped
- 4 spring onions, sliced
- 1 yellow or red pepper, cored, deseeded and chopped
- 2 small courgettes, finely sliced
- 1 small aubergine, cut into 2.5 cm (1 inch) cubes
- 6 small firm tomatoes, chopped
- 25 g (1 oz) walnuts or almonds, chopped
- 2 tablespoons balsamic vinegar
- salt and pepper
- chopped flat-leaf parsley, to garnish

1 Sandwich the venison steaks between sheets of greaseproof paper, then roll with a rolling pin to flatten them. Season with salt and pepper and rub in 1 tablespoon of the oil.

2 Heat the remaining oil in a deep frying pan, add the garlic, red onion and spring onions and stir-fry over a medium-high heat for 2 minutes. Add the remaining ingredients, except the venison, and cook over a medium heat for about 14 minutes until the vegetables are tender.

3 Meanwhile, cook the steaks under a preheated grill for 3–5 minutes on each side or until cooked to your liking. Wrap each steak in foil and leave to rest for 2–4 minutes.

4 Spoon a mound of the ratatouille on to 4 serving plates and top each with a steak. Serve garnished with chopped parsley.

Serves 4
Preparation time 15–20 minutes
Cooking time 25 minutes

Gado gado

- 175 g (6 oz) green beans, trimmed and cut into 5 cm (2 inch) lengths
- 175 g (6 oz) cauliflower, divided into florets
- 175 g (6 oz) broccoli, divided into florets
- 175 g (6 oz) cabbage, finely shredded
- 3 hard-boiled eggs, quartered
- 2 large tomatoes, quartered
- 1 large orange pepper, cored, deseeded and cut into thin slices
- 150 g (5 oz) cucumber, peeled and cut into chunky slices
- 125 g (4 oz) bean sprouts
- salt

Peanut sauce
- 450 ml (¾ pint) chicken or vegetable stock
- 125 g (4 oz) crunchy peanut butter
- 2 garlic cloves, finely chopped
- 1 spring onion, finely chopped
- ½ teaspoon chilli powder
- 1 tablespoon fish sauce
- 5 teaspoons lime juice

1 Bring a medium saucepan of water to the boil, add a little salt and keep at a gentle boil over a medium-high heat. Add the green beans and boil for 3 minutes or until they are just tender. Remove with a slotted spoon, place in a colander and refresh under cold running water. Place on a large serving plate.

2 Cook the cauliflower and broccoli for 2–3 minutes and refresh in the same way. Arrange in separate piles on the serving plate. Finally, cook the cabbage strips for 1 minute, drain and refresh under cold water. Add to the plate.

3 Arrange piles of egg, tomatoes, pepper, cucumber and bean sprouts on the plate. Cover with clingfilm and set aside.

4 To make the sauce, heat the stock in a saucepan until nearly boiling. Remove from the heat. Put the peanut butter in a separate pan with the garlic, spring onion and chilli powder. Gradually add the warm stock to the mixture, stirring continuously until thoroughly blended.

5 Add the fish sauce and lime juice to the sauce and bring to the boil. Reduce the heat to medium-low and simmer for 15 minutes, stirring occasionally, until thickened to a creamy consistency. Leave to cool slightly, then pour the warmed sauce over the vegetables and serve.

Serves 4
Preparation time 10 minutes
Cooking time 20–25 minutes

268
CALORIES
PER SERVING

Vegetable curry

- 1 tablespoon olive oil
- 1 onion, chopped
- 1 garlic clove, crushed
- 2 tablespoons medium curry paste
- 1.5 kg (3 lb) prepared vegetables, such as courgettes, peppers, squash, mushrooms and green beans
- 200 g (7 oz) can chopped tomatoes
- 400 ml (14 fl oz) can reduced-fat coconut milk
- 2 tablespoons chopped coriander

1 Heat the oil in a large saucepan, add the onion and garlic and fry for 2 minutes. Stir in the curry paste and fry for a further 1 minute.

2 Add the vegetables and fry for 2–3 minutes, stirring occasionally, then add the tomatoes and coconut milk. Stir well and bring to the boil, then reduce the heat and simmer for 12–15 minutes or until the vegetables are tender. Stir in the coriander and serve.

276
CALORIES
PER SERVING

Serves 4
Preparation time 20 minutes, plus marinating
Cooking time 40 minutes

Thai noodles with tofu

- 250 g (8 oz) tofu, diced
- 2 tablespoons dark soy sauce
- 1 teaspoon grated lime rind
- 175 g (6 oz) dried egg noodles
- 125 g (4 oz) button mushrooms, sliced
- 2 large carrots, cut into matchsticks
- 125 g (4 oz) sugar snap peas
- 125 g (4 oz) Chinese cabbage, shredded
- 2 tablespoons chopped coriander

Broth
- 1.8 litres (3 pints) vegetable stock
- 2 slices of fresh root ginger
- 2 garlic cloves
- 2 coriander sprigs
- 2 lemon grass stalks, crushed
- 1 red chilli, bruised

1 Mix together the tofu, soy sauce and lime rind in a shallow non-metallic dish. Leave to marinate for 30 minutes.

2 Meanwhile, make the broth. Put the vegetable stock in a large saucepan and add the ginger, garlic, coriander sprigs, lemon grass and chilli. Bring to the boil, then reduce the heat, cover and simmer for 30 minutes.

3 Strain the broth into another saucepan, return to the boil and plunge in the noodles. Add the mushrooms and tofu with any remaining marinade. Reduce the heat and simmer gently for 4 minutes.

4 Stir in the carrots, sugar snap peas, cabbage and chopped coriander and cook for a further 3–4 minutes. Serve immediately.

Serves 6
Preparation time 10 minutes
Cooking time 50 minutes

262
CALORIES
PER SERVING

Melanzane parmigiana

- 6 aubergines
- 1 tablespoon extra virgin olive oil
- 2 × 400 g (13 oz) cans chopped tomatoes
- 2 garlic cloves, crushed
- 250 g (8 oz) Cheddar cheese, grated
- 50 g (2 oz) Parmesan cheese, grated
- salt and pepper

1 Trim the aubergines and cut lengthways into thick slices. Brush them with the oil and place on 2 large baking sheets. Roast at the top of a preheated oven, 200°C (400°F), Gas Mark 6, for 10 minutes on each side until golden and tender.

2 Meanwhile, put the tomatoes and garlic in a saucepan and bring to the boil. Reduce the heat and simmer for 10 minutes, then season with salt and pepper.

3 Spoon a little of the tomato into an ovenproof dish and top with a layer of aubergines and some of the Cheddar. Continue with the layers, finishing with a layer of Cheddar on top. Sprinkle over the Parmesan and bake for 30 minutes until the cheese is bubbling and golden. Serve hot.

Serves 6
Preparation time 10 minutes
Cooking time 25–30 minutes

Butternut squash & ricotta frittata

- **1 tablespoon extra virgin rapeseed oil**
- **1 red onion, thinly sliced**
- **450 g (14½ oz) peeled and deseeded butternut squash, diced**
- **8 eggs**
- **2 tablespoons chopped sage**
- **1 tablespoon chopped thyme**
- **125 g (4 oz) ricotta cheese**
- **salt and pepper**

1 Heat the oil in a large, deep frying pan with an ovenproof handle over a medium-low heat, add the onion and butternut squash, then cover loosely and cook gently, stirring frequently, for 18–20 minutes until softened and golden.

2 Beat together the eggs, herbs and ricotta lightly in a jug, then season well with salt and pepper and pour over the squash mixture.

3 Cook for 2–3 minutes until the egg is almost set, stirring occasionally to prevent the base from burning.

4 Slide the pan under a preheated grill, keeping the handle away from the heat, and cook for 3–4 minutes until the egg is set and the frittata is golden. Slice into 6 wedges and serve hot.

Serves 4
Preparation time 20 minutes
Cooking time 25–30 minutes

293
CALORIES
PER SERVING

Artichoke pizza

- **30 cm (12 inch) ready-made pizza base**
- **6 canned artichoke hearts, drained**
- **handful of black olives**
- **6 strips of baked, smoked tofu**
- **125 g (4 oz) reduced-fat Cheddar or other hard cheese, grated (optional)**

Tomato topping
- **400 g (13 oz) can tomatoes**
- **1 onion, chopped**
- **2 garlic cloves, chopped**
- **1 teaspoon chopped oregano**
- **1 green pepper, cored, deseeded and chopped**
- **1 red pepper, cored, deseeded and chopped**
- **1 carrot, grated**
- **1 tablespoon olive oil**
- **1 tablespoon balsamic vinegar**
- **6 mushrooms, sliced**

1 To make the tomato topping, place the tomatoes in a blender or food processor and blend until smooth. Transfer to a large saucepan, add the onion, garlic and oregano and simmer gently for 20 minutes.

2 Stir the remaining topping ingredients into the pan, then pour the mixture over the pizza base, spreading it right to the edges. Arrange the remaining ingredients and cheese, if using, on top.

3 Place the pizza on a baking sheet and bake in a preheated oven, 200°C (400°F), Gas Mark 6, for 5–10 minutes or until the cheese begins to bubble and turn brown. Cut into 4 and serve.

Serves 4
Preparation time 10 minutes
Cooking time 20 minutes

Wild mushroom omelettes

- 2 tablespoons butter
- 200 g (7 oz) wild mushrooms, trimmed and sliced
- 8 large eggs, beaten
- 2 tablespoons chopped parsley
- 50 g (2 oz) Gruyère cheese, grated
- pepper

1 Melt a little of the butter in an omelette pan, add the mushrooms and sauté for 5–6 minutes until cooked and any moisture has evaporated. Remove the mushrooms from the pan.

2 Melt a little more butter in the same pan and add one-quarter of the beaten egg. Season well with pepper and stir with a wooden spoon, bringing the cooked egg to the centre of the pan and allowing the runny egg to flow to the edge of the pan and cook.

3 When there is only a little liquid egg left, sprinkle over a few mushrooms and some of the parsley and Gruyère. Fold the omelette over, tip on to a warm serving plate and keep warm. Repeat with the remaining ingredients to make 4 omelettes. Serve warm.

Serves 2
Preparation time 10 minutes
Cooking time 20–25 minutes

246
CALORIES
PER SERVING

Stuffed mushrooms

- 2 large, flat field mushrooms
- 2 tablespoons olive oil, plus extra for brushing
- 2 spring onions, chopped
- ½ red pepper, cored, deseeded and chopped
- 1 small courgette, chopped
- 4 pitted olives, chopped
- 2 tablespoons porridge oats
- 1 tablespoon chopped basil
- 1 tablespoon soy sauce
- 1 tablespoon lime juice
- salt and pepper

1 Wipe the mushrooms clean with damp kitchen paper, then remove the stalks and chop them.

2 Heat the oil in a small saucepan, add the chopped mushroom stalks, spring onions, red pepper, courgette, olives and oats and fry gently until the oats are golden. Stir in the basil, soy sauce and lime juice.

3 Brush the mushroom caps with oil and place on a baking sheet. Spoon the oat mixture on to the mushrooms and season with salt and pepper. Bake in a preheated oven, 180°C (350°F), Gas Mark 4, for 15–20 minutes until the caps begin to soften, then serve.

286
CALORIES
PER SERVING

Serves 6
Preparation time 5 minutes
Cooking time 30 minutes

Quick chickpea casserole

- 4 tablespoons olive oil
- 2 large onions, chopped
- 1–2 tablespoons ground cumin
- 4–5 garlic cloves, chopped
- 2 × 400 g (13 oz) cans chickpeas, rinsed and drained
- 300 ml (½ pint) vegetable stock
- juice of 1 lemon
- 500 g (1 lb) spinach leaves, roughly chopped
- salt and pepper

1 Heat the oil in a large saucepan, add the onions and sauté over a medium heat until softened. Add the cumin and garlic, stir and cook for 1 minute.

2 Add the chickpeas, stock and lemon juice, cover and simmer for 20 minutes. Add the spinach and season with salt and pepper. Mix well and cook for a further 7 minutes.

3 Serve hot, at room temperature or cold. The flavour improves if the casserole is left overnight.

Serves 8
Preparation time 15 minutes
Cooking time 25–30 minutes

273
CALORIES
PER SERVING

Veggie chilli

- 3 tablespoons olive oil
- 3 onions, chopped
- 4 garlic cloves, chopped
- 1 large green pepper, cored, deseeded and chopped
- 1 large red pepper, cored, deseeded and chopped
- 2 tablespoons mild chilli powder
- 2 tablespoons paprika
- 1 tablespoon ground cumin
- 1 bay leaf
- 2 teaspoons dried oregano
- 500 g (1 lb) fresh or canned tomatoes, chopped
- 750 ml (1¼ pint) vegetable stock
- 375 g (12 oz) canned kidney or borlotti beans, rinsed and drained
- salt and pepper

1 Heat the oil in a large saucepan, add the onions, garlic and red and green peppers and sauté over a medium heat for 2–3 minutes. Add the chilli powder, paprika and cumin and cook for a further 1 minute.

2 Add the remaining ingredients and bring to the boil, then reduce the heat and simmer for 20–25 minutes or until thickened. Season with salt and pepper and serve.

296
CALORIES
PER SERVING

Serves 6
Preparation time 10 minutes
Cooking time 30 minutes

Potato & onion tortilla

- 750 g (1½ lb) baking potatoes
- 4 tablespoons olive oil
- 2 large onions, thinly sliced
- 6 eggs, beaten
- salt and pepper

1 Slice the potatoes very thinly and toss them in a bowl with a little salt and pepper. Heat the oil in a medium-sized, heavy-based frying pan, add the potatoes and fry very gently for 10 minutes, turning frequently, until softened but not browned.

2 Add the onions and fry gently for a further 5 minutes without browning. Spread the potatoes and onions in an even layer in the pan and reduce the heat as low as possible.

3 Pour over the eggs, cover and cook very gently for about 15 minutes until the eggs have set. (If the centre of the omelette is too wet, place the pan under a preheated medium grill to finish cooking.) Tip the tortilla on to a plate, cut into 6 and serve warm or cold.

Serves 4
Preparation time 10 minutes
Cooking time 13–15 minutes

277
CALORIES
PER SERVING

Goats' cheese & herb soufflés

- **25 g (1 oz) polyunsaturated margarine**
- **50 g (2 oz) plain flour**
- **300 ml (½ pint) skimmed milk**
- **4 eggs, separated**
- **100 g (3½ oz) goats' cheese, crumbled**
- **1 tablespoon chopped mixed herbs, such as parsley, chives and thyme**
- **1 tablespoon grated Parmesan cheese**
- **75 g (3 oz) rocket leaves**
- **2 tablespoons fat-free salad dressing**
- **salt and pepper**

1 Melt the margarine in a medium saucepan, add the flour and cook, stirring, for 1 minute. Gradually add the milk, whisking all the time, and cook for 2 minutes until the roux has thickened.

2 Remove the pan from the heat. Beat in the egg yolks one at a time, then stir in the goats' cheese. Season well with salt and pepper.

3 Whisk the egg whites in a large bowl until they form firm peaks, then gradually fold them into the cheese mixture with the herbs. Transfer to 4 lightly oiled ramekins, sprinkle over the Parmesan, then bake in a preheated oven, 190°C (375°F), Gas Mark 5, for 10–12 minutes until risen and golden.

4 Toss together the rocket and dressing in a bowl and serve with the soufflés.

Serves 4
Preparation time 10 minutes
Cooking time 15–18 minutes

Chocolate & raspberry soufflés

- 100 g (3½ oz) plain dark chocolate, broken into squares
- 3 eggs, separated
- 50 g (2 oz) self-raising flour, sifted
- 40 g (1½ oz) caster sugar
- 150 g (5 oz) raspberries
- icing sugar, for dusting

1 Put the chocolate in a large heatproof bowl and melt over a saucepan of gently simmering water.

2 Remove from the heat and leave to cool slightly, then whisk in the egg yolks. Fold in the flour.

3 Whisk the egg whites and caster sugar in a medium clean bowl until they form soft peaks. Beat a spoonful of the egg whites into the chocolate mixture to loosen it up before gently folding in the rest.

4 Divide the raspberries between 4 lightly greased ramekins, pour over the chocolate mixture, then bake in a preheated oven, 190°C (375°F), Gas Mark 5, for 12–15 minutes until the soufflés have risen.

5 Dust with icing sugar and serve immediately.

Serves 6
Preparation time 20 minutes
Cooking time 25–30 minutes

250
CALORIES
PER SERVING

Apple & fig crumble

- **125g (4 oz) wholemeal plain flour**
- **50 g (2 oz) brown sugar**
- **50 g (2 oz) unsaturated spread**
- **500 g (1 lb) cooking apples, such as Bramleys, peeled, cored and sliced**
- **6 dried or fresh figs, diced**
- **grated rind and juice of 1 lemon**
- **1 teaspoon ground cinnamon**

1 Sift the flour into a large bowl, add the unsaturated spread and lightly rub in with the fingertips until the mixture resembles coarse crumbs. Stir in the sugar.

2 Place the fruit in a 1.2 litre (2 pint) ovenproof dish. Add the lemon rind and juice and cinnamon. Spoon the crumble mixture over the fruit and bake in a preheated oven, 180°C (350°F), Gas Mark 4, for 25–30 minutes until golden brown. Serve warm.

Top tip

The average food craving lasts about 10 minutes, so try to distract yourself to get past your hunger pang. Make yourself a cup of herbal tea, have a bath or phone a friend.

Calorie counter

	Average portion (g)	Calories
FRUIT		
Apples (weighed whole with core)		
Cox's Pippin	125	53
Golden Delicious	125	50
Granny Smith	125	52
Apples (stewed with sugar)	110	81
Apricots (flesh only)	80	25
Avocado (flesh only)	140	266
Bananas	100	95
Blackberries	100	25
Blueberries	50	35
Cherries (weighed with stones)	80	31
Clementines (weighed with peel and pips)	80	22
Figs	55	24
Fruit Salad	140	77
Grapefruit (weighed with peel and pips)	170	20
Grapes	100	60
Kiwifruit (weighed with skin)	75	32
Lemon, unpeeled	60	8
Lime, unpeeled	40	4
Melon (weighed with skin)		
Cantaloupe	180	23
Galia	200	30
Honeydew	200	38
Nectarines (weighed with skin)	150	54
Oranges (weighed with skin)	200	52
Papaya (flesh only)	140	50
Peaches (weighed with stone)	150	45
Pears (weighed whole with core)	150	54
Pineapple	80	33
Plums (weighed with stone)	70	24
Raspberries	60	15
Satsumas (weighed with skin)	87	23
Strawberries	100	27
Watermelon (flesh only)	200	62
DRIED FRUIT, NUTS AND SEEDS		
Almonds	15	91
Apricots, dried	32	60
Brazil Nuts	10	68
Cashew Nuts	10	63
Cashew Nuts, roasted and salted	25	153
Chestnuts	50	85
Cranberries, dried, sweetened	25	82
Dates, dried, pitted	50	35
Figs, ready-to-eat	20	68
Hazelnuts	10	65
Mixed Nuts	40	243
Mixed Nuts and Raisins	40	192
Peanuts, plain	13	73
Peanuts, dry-roasted	40	236
Pecan Nuts	20	138
Pine Nuts	5	34
Pistachio Nuts, roasted and salted	10	60
Prunes, dried	66	93
Pumpkin Seeds	16	91
Raisins, seedless	25	76
Sultanas	25	73
Sunflower Seeds	16	96
Walnuts	20	138

	Average portion (g)	Calories
VEGETABLES (RAW, PREPARED, UNLESS OTHERWISE STATED)		
Asparagus	125	33
Aubergine (grilled)	100	75
Beans		
Broad	120	58
French	90	20
Runner	90	16
Beetroot	40	18
Broccoli	85	20
Brussels Sprouts	90	32
Cabbage		
Red	90	14
Savoy	95	16
White	95	13
Carrots	60	14
Cauliflower	90	25
Celery	30	2
Chilli Peppers	10	3
Corn on the Cob (weighed whole)	200	123
Courgettes	90	17
Cucumber	23	2
Fennel	100	11
Leeks	75	16
Lettuce	80	13
Mushrooms	80	10
Onions	150	54
Parsnips	65	43
Peas	70	55
Peppers		
Green	160	24
Red	160	51
Yellow	160	42
Potatoes		
New (boiled)	175	116
Old (baked)	180	245
Old (boiled)	175	126
Old (mashed with butter)	120	122
Old (roasted)	130	151
Radishes	48	6
Spinach	90	23
Spring Onions	10	2
Squash (baked)	65	21
Swede	60	7
Sweet Potato (baked)	130	150
Sweetcorn	60	14
Tomatoes	85	14
Tomatoes (grilled)	85	42
Tomatoes, Cherry	90	16
CHEESE		
Brie	40	144
Camembert	40	116
Cheddar	40	166
Cheese Spread	30	81
Cottage, 4% fat	40	36
Cottage, 2% fat	40	28
Danish Blue	30	103
Dolcelatte	40	158
Double Gloucester	40	165
Edam	40	136
Emmental	40	160
Feta	50	125
Gouda	40	151

	Average portion (g)	Calories
Halloumi	40	124
Mozzarella, fresh	55	141
Mozzarella, grated	55	164
Paneer	40	130
Parmesan, freshly grated	20	82
Red Leicester	40	161
Ricotta	55	79
Roquefort	28	105
Soft light	30	47
Soft medium fat	30	74
Stilton	35	143

EGGS

Boiled	50	74
Fried	60	107
Poached	50	74
Omelette, Cheese (2 eggs)	150	399
Omelette, Plain (2 eggs)	120	180
Omelette, Spanish (2 eggs)	150	229
Scrambled, no milk (2 eggs)	100	160
Scrambled, with milk (2 eggs)	120	296

DAIRY

Crème fraîche	50	190
Crème fraîche, low fat	50	85
Fromage frais, fruit	100	135
Fromage frais, fruit, virtually fat-free	100	50
Fromage frais, natural	100	113
Fromage frais, natural, virtually fat-free	100	48
Greek Yogurt, 0%	100	57
Milk		
Goats' Milk	146	88
Semi-skimmed Milk	146	67
Skimmed Milk	146	48
Soya Milk	146	47
Whole Milk	146	96

MEAT

Beef

Braising Steak (braised)	140	315
Braising Steak (slow-cooked)	140	276
Fillet Steak (grilled)	168	316
Mince, extra lean (stewed)	140	248
Rump Steak (grilled)	163	287
Rump Steak strips (stir-fried)	103	214
Sirloin Steak (grilled)	166	292
Lamb		
Leg Steaks (grilled)	90	178
Loin Chops (grilled)	70	149
Mince (stewed)	90	187
Rack of Lamb (roasted)	90	203
Shoulder Joint (roasted)	90	212
Stewing (stewed)	130	312
Offal		
Liver, Lambs' (fried)	100	237
Liver, Ox (stewed)	70	139
Liver, Pig (stewed)	70	132
Livers, Chicken (fried)	70	118
Pork, Bacon and Ham		
Bacon		
Collar Joint (boiled)	46	88
Loin Steaks (grilled)	100	191
Rashers, Back (dry-fried)	100	295

	Average portion (g)	Calories
Rashers, Back (grilled)	100	214
Rashers, Back, dry-cured (grilled)	100	257
Rashers, Back, smoked (grilled)	100	293
Rashers, Back, sweet cure (grilled)	100	258
Rashers, Middle (grilled)	100	307
Rashers, Streaky (grilled)	100	337
Fillet of Pork (grilled)	120	240
Gammon		
Joint (boiled)	170	347
Rashers (grilled)	100	199
Ham		
Ham, Parma	47	105
Ham, premium	56	74
Pork Shoulder, cured	100	103
Leg Joint (roasted)	90	164
Loin Chops (grilled)	75	140
Loin Joint (pot-roasted)	90	177
Loin Steaks (fried)	120	229
Mince (stewed)	90	172
Pork, diced (stewed)	90	166
Pork Steaks (grilled)	135	228
Spare Rib (grilled)	110	321
Spare Rib Joint (pot-roasted)	90	181

POULTRY AND GAME

Chicken		
Breast, skinless (grilled)	130	192
Breast strips (stir-fried)	90	145
Drumsticks, skinned (casseroled)	47	87
Drumsticks, skinned (roasted)	47	71
Leg Quarter (roasted)	146	345
Leg Quarter, skinned (casseroled)	146	257
Thighs, skinless, boneless (casseroled)	45	81
Wings (grilled)	100	274
Duck (roasted)	185	361
Goose (roasted)	185	590
Grouse (roasted)	160	205
Pheasant (roasted)	160	352
Pigeon (roasted)	115	215
Rabbit (stewed)	160	182
Turkey		
Breast, skinless (grilled)	90	140
Drumsticks, skinned (roasted)	90	146
Mince (stewed)	90	158
Strips (stir-fried)	90	148
Thighs, diced skinless, boneless (casseroled)	90	163
Venison (roasted)	120	198

FISH AND SEAFOOD

Anchovies, in oil	10	28
Cod (baked)	120	115
Cod (poached)	120	113
Cod (steamed)	120	100
Cod, Smoked (poached)	120	121
Crab (boiled, dressed in shell)	130	166
Crab, in brine	40	31
Haddock (grilled)	120	125
Haddock (poached)	120	136
Haddock (steamed)	120	107
Haddock, Smoked (poached)	150	201
Hake (grilled)	100	113
Halibut (grilled)	145	175
Halibut (poached)	110	169

	Average portion (g)	Calories
Halibut (steamed)	110	144
Kipper (baked)	130	267
Kipper (grilled)	130	332
Lobster (boiled, dressed in shell)	250	258
Mackerel (grilled)	147	351
Monkfish (grilled)	70	67
Mussels (boiled, shelled)	40	42
Plaice (grilled)	130	125
Prawns (boiled, shelled)	60	59
Salmon (grilled)	82	176
Salmon (steamed)	77	152
Salmon, Smoked	56	80
Sardines (grilled)	40	78
Scallops (steamed, shelled)	70	83
Swordfish (grilled)	125	174
Trout, Brown (steamed)	155	209
Trout, Rainbow (steamed)	155	209
Tuna, canned in brine	45	45
Tuna, raw	45	61

RICE, PASTA AND PULSES (UNCOOKED, UNLESS OTHERWISE STATED)

	Average portion (g)	Calories
Bulgar Wheat	100	338
Butter Beans, canned	100	77
Butter Beans, dried (boiled)	100	103
Cannellini Beans, canned	100	87
Chickpeas, canned	100	115
Chickpeas, dried (boiled)	100	121
Couscous	100	364
Lentils, Puy-style, canned	100	118
Lentils, Puy-style, dried (boiled)	100	105
Kidney Beans, canned	100	100
Macaroni (boiled)	125	108
Noodles, Egg (boiled)	125	78
Noodles (fried)	125	191
Rice		
Brown (boiled)	125	176
White, glutinous (boiled)	125	82
White, polished (boiled)	125	154
Spaghetti (boiled)	125	130
Spaghetti, wholemeal (boiled)	125	141

BREAD

	Average portion (g)	Calories
Ciabatta, plain	50	135
Croissants	60	224
Crumpets	40	83
Focaccia	50	147
French Baguette	40	109
Garlic Bread	20	73
Hot Cross Buns	50	155
Muffins, English, white	68	152
Pitta Bread	75	191
Rolls		
Brown	48	113
White, crusty	50	131
White, soft	45	114
Wholemeal	48	117
Sliced		
Brown	36	83
Granary	36	92
White	40	94
Wholemeal	40	93
Soda Bread, brown	130	267
Tortilla, soft	160	451

	Average portion (g)	Calories
CEREALS		
Bran Flakes	30	95
Bran Strands	40	104
Corn Flakes	30	108
Frosted Flakes	30	113
Fruit and Fibre	40	147
Hoops, Honey	30	111
Muesli	50	184
Oat Flakes	30	107
Porridge, with milk and water	160	133
Porridge, with water	160	78
Porridge, with whole milk	160	186
Puffed Wheat	20	64
Rice Pops	30	111
Wheat, shredded	45	150
Wheat, shredded, mini	45	154
Wholewheat Biscuits	38	134
JAMS AND SPREADS		
Honey	16	91
Jam	15	39
Lemon Curd	15	42
Marmalade	15	26
Meat Extract	8	14
Peanut Butter, crunchy	25	152
Peanut Butter, smooth	25	156
Yeast Extract	4	9
DIPS		
Guacamole	45	58
Hummus	30	56
Taramasalata	45	227
Tzatziki	45	30
COLD DRINKS AND JUICES		
Apple Juice	160	61
Carrot Juice	160	38
Cola	160	66
Cola, diet	160	Trace
Grapefruit Juice	160	53
Lemonade	160	35
Lemonade, diet	160	Trace
Orange Juice, fresh	160	53
Pineapple Juice	160	66
Pomegranate Juice	160	70
HOT DRINKS		
Cappuccino, with semi-skimmed milk	190	46
Coffee, with semi-skimmed milk	190	13
Coffee, with skimmed milk	190	8
Coffee, with whole milk	190	15
Hot Chocolate, with semi-skimmed milk	190	135
Hot Chocolate, with skimmed milk	190	112
Hot Chocolate, with whole milk	190	171
Latte, with semi-skimmed milk	190	60
Latte, with skimmed milk	190	33
Latte, with whole milk	190	85
Tea, black	190	Trace
Tea, Chinese	190	2
Tea, green	190	Trace
Tea, herbal	190	2
Tea, with semi-skimmed milk	190	13
Tea, with skimmed milk	190	8
Tea, with whole milk	190	15

Index

Acknowledgements

Publisher: Sarah Ford
Managing Editor: Clare Churly
Designer: Eoghan O'Brien
Layouts by Jeremy Tiltson
Senior Production Manager: Peter Hunt